JavaScript Interview Questions, Answers, and Explanations

By Terry Sanchez

JavaScript Interview Questions, Answers, and Explanations

ISBN 13 978-1-933804-56-9
ISBN 1-933804-56-4

Compiled by Terry Sanchez
Edited by Emilee Newman Bowles

Printed in the United States of America

Please visit our website at www.sapcookbook.com

Table of Contents

Question 1: Image Loop

I have a problem with the codes below:

```
<html>
<body>
<script type="text/JavaScript">
function curl(a){
var i = 1
if (a.substring(0,7)!='http://' ||
a.substring(a.length-3,a.length)!='gif')
{
alert("Error");
}
else
{
document.getElementById('dply').innerHTML='';
for (i = 1; i < 6; i++){
a=a.replace("*n*",i);
document.getElementById('dply').innerHTML =
document.getElementById('dply').innerHTML +
'<br>'+'<img src="'+a+'"> <a href="'+a+'">'+a+'</a>';
  }
 }
}
</script>
<input type="text" id="url" size="40"
value="http://www.eastman.ucl.ac.uk/guide/*n*.gif">
<input type="button"
onclick="curl(document.getElementById('url').value)">
<div id="dply">
</div>
</body>
</html>
```

Why does the script above not go from 1.gif to 2.gif, 3.gif, 4.gif and 5.gif?

A: When you call the function with the value http://www.eastman.ucl.ac.uk/guide/*n*.gif, the parameter a takes this value.

In the first iteration, when i has the value 1, the statement a=a.replace("*n*",i); changes the value of a to http://www.eastman.ucl.ac.uk/guide/1.gif.

In the next iterations, when i has the value 2, 3, 4 ... the statement a=a.replace("*n*",i); will do nothing, because the string *n* is no longer part of a. The value of a (http://www.eastman.ucl.ac.uk/guide/1.gif) will remain unchanged.

The script should be:

```
<html>
<body>
<script type="text/JavaScript">
function curl(a) {
var i = 1
if (a.substring(0,7)!='http://' ||
a.substring(a.length-3,a.length)!='gif')
{
    alert("Error");
    }
    else
        {
        document.getElementById('dply').innerHTML='';
        for (i = 1; i < 6; i++)
        {
            b=a;
            b=b.replace("*n*",i);
            document.getElementById('dply').innerHTML
= document.getElementById('dply').innerHTML +
        '<br>'+'<img src="'+b+'"> <a
href="'+b+'">'+b+'</a>';
        }
    }
}
</script>
<input type="text" id="url" size="40"
value="http://www.eastman.ucl.ac.uk/guide/*n*.gif">
<input type="button"
onclick="curl(document.getElementById('url').value)">
<div id="dply">
</div>
</body>
</html>
```

Inserting the statement b=a; allows the parameter a to always keep the initial value and the string *n* will be found and replaced with 2, 3, 4, and 5.

Question 2: Autoredirect

I am using PHP to explore the referring URL and then putting that as the location. The redirect code is as follows:

```
$Refer[3] = "newequip.php?ClientName=$ClientNameF";
echo "<html><head><title>Add Equipment
Results</title></head><body
onload=setTimeout(\"location.href='\\".$Refer[3]."'\"
,2500)>";
```

When I load it from the page already formatted with the ClientName in the URL, it redirects perfectly. I had it formatted by replacing the spaces with %20. The server side code from this page is as follows:

```
<body
onload=setTimeout("location.href='\equipinfo.php?Clie
ntName=Fox%20Theatre%20Hill&EquipName=T2'",2500)>
```

However, when I try to do the same from the other page, which needs to be sent back with the ClientName, it is not working. The client side code from this other page is as follows:

```
<body
onload=setTimeout("location.href='\newequip.php?Clien
tName=Fox%20Theatre%20Hill'",2500)>
```

Why does it work for one page but not for the other?

A: To make it work in both server and client side, edit the statement location
.href='\newequip.php?ClientName=Fox%2oTheatre%2oHill'

The backslash n (\n) makes a new line in JavaScript. If you're using this on a web server, use a forward slash instead.

Question 3: Selectbox onchange Disable Other Selectbox

I have two select boxes, but I only want the user to be able to select one of them. Both boxes are dynamic and populate data from recordsets.

Both boxes should be initially enabled. Once the user makes a selection in one of the boxes, the other should become disabled. If the user changes his mind and wants to select the other box, he should be able to select the first option (Option 0) in the box to re-enable the other box.

The following is a sample code for select boxes to start with:

```
<html>
<head>
</head>
<body>
<form name="frmFilter">
  <select name="lstCounty" id="lstCounty"
onChange="">
        <option selected value="0">By
County...</option>
        <option value="1">Other option 1</option>
        <option value="2">Other option 2</option>
  </select>
  <select name="lstCity" id="lstCity" onChange="">
        <option selected value="0">By City...</option>
        <option value="1">Other option 1</option>
        <option value="2">Other option 2</option>
  </select>
</form>
</body>
</html>
```

How do I write a code that will allow the user to select only one box?

A: This can probably be done in a more compact bit of code, but the following may be easier to understand and quicker than waiting for a difficult-to-read function.

```
function chgSelect(which) {
  if (which == 'County') {
    if
(document.getElementById('lstCounty').selectedIndex
== 0) //Unlock lstCity
      document.getElementById('lstCity').disabled =
false;
    else // lock city
      document.getElementById('lstCity').disabled =
true;
  }
  else {
    if
(document.getElementById('lstCity').selectedIndex ==
0) //Unlock lstCounty
      document.getElementById('lstCounty').disabled =
false;
    else // lock lstCounty
      document.getElementById('lstCounty').disabled =
true;
  }
}

<form name="frmFilter">
  <select name="lstCounty" id="lstCounty"
onChange="chgSelect('County');">
      <option selected value="0">By
County...</option>
      <option value="1">Other option 1</option>
      <option value="2">Other option 2</option>
  </select>
  <select name="lstCity" id="lstCity"
onChange="chgSelect('City');">
      <option selected value="0">By City...</option>
      <option value="1">Other option 1</option>
      <option value="2">Other option 2</option>
  </select>
</form>
```

Question 4: Dynamic URL Links

I have a JavaScript loop that gets a user's settings, from which I would like to dynamically create the user's html links on a web page. For example, the user selects certain companies. I will then create links to the companies he selected. How do I dynamically generate html links for a list of 5 to 10 items?

A: Two of the many ways to dynamically generate html links are the following:

```
document.write('<a href="something.html">link</a>');
```

or

```
document.getElementById('linkContainer').innerHTML =
'<a href="something.html">link</a>';

<div id="linkContainer"></div>
```

Question 5: Can't Find Error in Simple JavaScript

When I have the following JavaScript in my file and try to execute a function defined after it, the function is never executed. When I remove this piece, it works fine.

```
function findOffset(alphabet, ch)
{
    var findOffset = alphabet.indexOf(ch) - 1

    If (findOffset == -1) {
        return -5
    } else {
        return findOffset
    }
}
```

The part that gives me trouble is the If ... Else statement. I have included the rest of the code to put it into context.

Is there something wrong with the above code?

A: Change the capital I in If to a lowercase i and rename the variable (it should not have the same name as the function).

Your logic has a flaw in it, too. Because you subtract 1 from the index of a character, you could get a value of -2, if the character you're checking for is not in the string c alled alphabet.

Putting some semicolon terminators in wouldn't go amiss either.

Question 6: String Split

I am using split() function on a string like this:

```
var words = s.value.split(" ");
```

but the above statement only splits on a blank space. I also want to split on ":" and "-".

The following statement didn't work either:

```
var words = s.value.split(" |:|-");
```

How do I write the statement?

A: Suppose one takes it for granted that s.value is a string. Then you can write the statement like this:

```
var words = s.value.split(/ |:|-/);
```

The left-hand-side words are treated as an array.

Question 7: IE6 dhtml JavaScript Error

I am trying to show/hide a table cell using the display property. My code is as follows:

```
function toggleId(id){
    try {
        var elem = document.getElementById(id);
        if (elem.style.display != 'table-cell'){
            elem.style.display = 'table-cell';
        } else {
            elem.style.display = 'none';
        }
    } catch (e) {//fail gracefully
        str = "";
        for (i in e)
            str += e[i] + "\\n";
        alert(str);
        alert(elem.style.display);
    }
}
```

The above function is called by the following code:

```
    <td class="rowOdd">
        <a href="" onclick="toggleId('row_f'); return
false;">Edit</a><br />
    </td>
    </tr>    <tr>
        <td colspan="5"  id="row_f"
style="display:none;">
        <form name="edit_f" method="POST" action="">

        </form>
        </td>
    </tr>
```

It works perfectly in FF, but fails completely in IE.

I get the following error message:

Could not get the display property. Invalid argument.

The line highlighted in bold is the one IE points to as broken. I don't get any error message when I remove the said line.

How do I correct this error?

A: You can keep your table cells for browsers that support them, and still get IE working with some neat CSS tricks:

1. Make sure your document is in "quirks mode" by placing a comment on the line before your DOCTYPE (or simply removing your DOCTYPE altogether, b ut I wouldn't recommend this).

2. For IE only, you can then use floats and heights of 100% to emulate table cells and rows.

Or try giving it a display of " instead of 'table-cell' and see what happens.

Question 8: Client Side Calculating a Form

I have an html page with the following code. It asks six questions, scores them, and keeps a running total in the second to the last textbox.

```
<html>
<head>
<title></title>
<script language="JavaScript" type="text/JavaScript">
<!--
function zxcSubTotal(obj,id,tid){
zxct=document.getElementById(tid);
if (!zxct.ary){ zxct.ary=new Array(); }
zxccbs=obj.getElementsByTagName('INPUT');
for (zxc0=0;zxc0<zxccbs.length;zxc0++){
if
(zxccbs[zxc0].type=='checkbox'&&zxccbs[zxc0].checked)
{
document.getElementById(id).value=zxccbs[zxc0].value;
if (!zxccbs[zxc0].set){
```

```
zxccbs[zxc0].set=true;
zxct.ary[zxct.ary.length]=zxccbs[zxc0];
}
}
}
zxcv=0
for (zxc1=0;zxc1<zxct.ary.length;zxc1++){
if (zxct.ary[zxc1].checked){
zxcv+=parseFloat(zxct.ary[zxc1].value);
}
}
zxct.value=zxcv;
}

</script>
</head>
<body onload="f6_OneCheckBox()">
<table border="1">
<TR><TD colspan="3"><table width="100%">
<TR><TD align='center'> <TD align='center'>P<TD
align='center'>F</TD></TR>
</Table>
<tr onclick="zxcSubTotal(this,'Group1','Total');">
<td>1.
<td><input title="f6_Group1" type="checkbox"
value="1"></td>
<td><input title="f6_Group1" type="checkbox"
value="0"></td>
<input id="Group1"type="hidden" name=""></td>
</tr>
<tr onclick="zxcSubTotal(this,'Group2','Total');">
<td>2.
<td><input title="f6_Group2" type="checkbox"
value="1" name=""></td>
<td><input title="f6_Group2" type="checkbox"
value="0" name=""></td>
<input id="Group2"type="hidden" name=""></td>
</tr>
<tr onclick="zxcSubTotal(this,'Group3','Total');">
<td>3.
<td><input title="f6_Group3" type="checkbox"
value="1" name=""></td>
<td><input title="f6_Group3" type="checkbox"
value="0" name=""></td>
<input id="Group3"type="hidden" name=""></td>
</tr>
<tr onclick="zxcSubTotal(this,'Group4','Total');">
<td>4.
<td><input title="f6_Group4" type="checkbox"
value="1" name=""></td>
```

```html
<td><input title="f6_Group4" type="checkbox"
value="0" name=""></td>
<input id="Group4"type="hidden" name=""></td>
</tr>

<tr onclick="zxcSubTotal(this,'Group5','Total');">
<td>5.
<td><input title="f6_Group5" type="checkbox"
value="1" name=""></td>
<td><input title="f6_Group5" type="checkbox"
value="0" name=""></td>
<input id="Group5"type="hidden" name=""></td>
</tr>

<tr onclick="zxcSubTotal(this,'Group6','Total');">
<td>6.
<td><input title="f6_Group6" type="checkbox"
value="1" name=""></td>
<td><input title="f6_Group6" type="checkbox"
value="0" name=""></td>
<input id="Group6"type="hidden" name=""></td>
</tr>

<tr >
<td colspan=3 ><input id="Total"type="text"
name="total" size=5 ></td>
</tr>
<TR><TD colspan="3"><INPUT type="text" size="5"
name="passfail">
</table>

<script language="JavaScript" type="text/JavaScript">
<!--
function f6_OneCheckBox(){
f6_cbs=document.getElementsByTagName('INPUT');
for (f6_0=0;f6_0<f6_cbs.length;f6_0++){
if (f6_cbs[f6_0].title.substring(0,3)=='f6_'){
f6_cbs[f6_0].onclick=function(){
f6_CheckOnlyOne(this); }
}
}
}
function f6_CheckOnlyOne(f6_){
for (f6_0=0;f6_0<f6_cbs.length;f6_0++){
if
(f6_cbs[f6_0].title==f6_.title&&f6_cbs[f6_0]!=f6_){
f6_cbs[f6_0].checked=false;
}
}
```

```
}
</script>
</body>
</html>
```

How do I add a pass or fail text in the last textbox (named passfail) if the total score is below 4 or if questions 2 or 4 are marked "F"?

A: This does what you want. I commented the changes; you can leave them in or take them out. It works either way. Assign IDs that you want, just remember to change them in the if/else statement.

```
<html>
<head>
<title></title>
<script language="JavaScript" type="text/JavaScript">
<!--
function zxcSubTotal(obj,id,tid){
zxct=document.getElementById(tid);
if (!zxct.ary){ zxct.ary=new Array(); }
zxccbs=obj.getElementsByTagName('INPUT');
for (zxc0=0;zxc0<zxccbs.length;zxc0++){
if
(zxccbs[zxc0].type=='checkbox'&&zxccbs[zxc0].checked)
{
document.getElementById(id).value=zxccbs[zxc0].value;
if (!zxccbs[zxc0].set){
zxccbs[zxc0].set=true;
zxct.ary[zxct.ary.length]=zxccbs[zxc0];
}
}
}
zxcv=0
for (zxc1=0;zxc1<zxct.ary.length;zxc1++){
if (zxct.ary[zxc1].checked){
zxcv+=parseFloat(zxct.ary[zxc1].value);
}
}
zxct.value=zxcv;
<!--Start new code-->
if ((zxcv < 4) ||
(document.getElementById("2f").checked) ||
(document.getElementById("4f").checked)){
document.getElementById("passfail").value = "Fail"
}
else {
```

```
document.getElementById("passfail").value = "Pass"
}
<!--End new code-->
}

</script>
</head>
<body onload="f6_OneCheckBox()">
<table border="1">
<TR><TD colspan="3"><table width="100%">
<TR><TD align='center'> <TD align='center'>P<TD
align='center'>F</TD></TR>
</Table>
<tr onclick="zxcSubTotal(this,'Group1','Total');">
<td>1.
<td><input title="f6_Group1" type="checkbox"
value="1"></td>
<td><input title="f6_Group1" type="checkbox"
value="0"></td>
<input id="Group1"type="hidden" name=""></td>
</tr>
<tr onclick="zxcSubTotal(this,'Group2','Total');">
<td>2.
<td><input title="f6_Group2" type="checkbox"
value="1" name=""></td>
<!--Assign id to this td-->
<td><input title="f6_Group2" type="checkbox"
value="0" name="" id="2f"></td>
<input id="Group2"type="hidden" name=""></td>
</tr>
<tr onclick="zxcSubTotal(this,'Group3','Total');">
<td>3.
<td><input title="f6_Group3" type="checkbox"
value="1" name=""></td>
<td><input title="f6_Group3" type="checkbox"
value="0" name=""></td>
<input id="Group3"type="hidden" name=""></td>
</tr>
<tr onclick="zxcSubTotal(this,'Group4','Total');">
<td>4.
<td><input title="f6_Group4" type="checkbox"
value="1" name=""></td>
<!--Assign id to this td-->
<td><input title="f6_Group4" type="checkbox"
value="0" name="" id="4f"></td>
<input id="Group4"type="hidden" name=""></td>
</tr>

<tr onclick="zxcSubTotal(this,'Group5','Total');">
```

```
<td>5.
<td><input title="f6_Group5" type="checkbox"
value="1" name=""></td>
<td><input title="f6_Group5" type="checkbox"
value="0" name=""></td>
<input id="Group5"type="hidden" name=""></td>
</tr>

<tr onclick="zxcSubTotal(this,'Group6','Total');">
<td>6.
<td><input title="f6_Group6" type="checkbox"
value="1" name=""></td>
<td><input title="f6_Group6" type="checkbox"
value="0" name=""></td>
<input id="Group6"type="hidden" name=""></td>
</tr>

<tr >
<td colspan=3 ><input id="Total"type="text"
name="total" size=5 onChange="result()"></td>
</tr>
<TR><!--Closed td and tr assigned id to this td and
set initial value to start--><TD colspan="3"><INPUT
type="text" size="5" name="passfail" id="passfail"
value="Start"></td>
</tr>
</table>

<script language="JavaScript" type="text/JavaScript">
<!--
function f6_OneCheckBox(){
f6_cbs=document.getElementsByTagName('INPUT');
for (f6_0=0;f6_0<f6_cbs.length;f6_0++){
if (f6_cbs[f6_0].title.substring(0,3)=='f6_'){
f6_cbs[f6_0].onclick=function(){
f6_CheckOnlyOne(this); }
}
}
}
function f6_CheckOnlyOne(f6_){
for (f6_0=0;f6_0<f6_cbs.length;f6_0++){
if
(f6_cbs[f6_0].title==f6_.title&&f6_cbs[f6_0]!=f6_){
f6_cbs[f6_0].checked=false;
}
}
}
</script>
</body>
</html>
```

Question 9: Radio Buttons

I am trying to get values from radio buttons using the following code:

```
<!DOCTYPE HTML PUBLIC "-//W3C//DTD HTML 4.0
Transitional//EN">
<html>
<head>
  <title></title>
<script type="text/JavaScript">
<!--
function Validate(){
var Tile;
for (i = 0; i < document.form1.Tile.length; i++){
alert ("I: " + Tile[i]);
if (document.form1.Tile[i].checked == true){
Tile = document.form1.Tile[i].value;
alert ("Tile: " + Tile);
}
}
return false;
}
//-->
</script>
</head>
<body>
<FORM name="form1">
<img height="90" src="tiles/marble.jpg" width="60"
border="0"><br>
     <input name="Tile" type="radio"
value="marble">Marble
<img height="90" src="tiles/wood.jpg" width="60"
align="top" border="0"><br>
     <input name="Tile" type="radio"
value="wood">Wood<p />

<p><input type="submit" onClick="Validate()"></p>
</body>
</html>
```

I put the alerts in there just to see what is going on but they don't pop either.

How do I make it work?

A: Put your validation function in the <form> instead, like this:

```
<FORM name="form1" onsubmit="return Validate();">
```

This line:

```
alert ("I: " + Tile[i]);
```

will cause an error because the Tile variable isn't an array, the function will terminate at that point, and the form will submit without error checking. You may be after something like this instead:

```
alert('I: ' + document.form1.Tile[i].checked);
```

Since you always return false from the function, it will never submit. Use this instead:

```
if (document.form1.Tile[i].checked == true)
   {
   Tile = document.form1.Tile[i].value;
   alert ("Tile: " + Tile);
   return true;
   }
```

You also might look into learning to format your code with indents to make it more readable. The few bytes you save by not indenting will save far less time than what it takes to read and figure out what goes with what and where.

Question 10: Launch a Pop-up Window from Form

I am trying to pass into a function the height, width, scrolling Boolean and, if necessary, the URL. I need the following code to be versatile so that it can be used on a "Print Page" feature and a couple others on the site.

```
function newWindow(w, h, scroll, window, url) {
    var winl = (screen.width - w) / 2;
    var wint = (screen.height - h) / 2;
        winprops = '+url+', '+window+', 'toolbar=no,
location=no, directories=no, status=no, menubar=no,
height='+h+', width='+w+', top='+wint+',
left='+winl+', scrollbars='+scroll+', resizable=yes';
        win = window.open(winprops);
        if (parseInt(navigator.appVersion) >= 4) {
        win.window.focus();
    }
}
```

The HTML, which is actually generated from a PHP page, has this:

```
<form target='paypal'
action='https://www.paypal.com/cgi-bin/webscr'
method='post'>
<input type='hidden' name='cmd' value='_cart'>
<input type='hidden' name='business'
value='myemail@mysite.com'>
<input type='hidden' name='item_name' value='myitem'>
<input type='hidden' name='item_number' value='7B'>
<input type='hidden' name='amount' value='50'>
<input type='hidden' name='currency_code'
value='USD'>
<input type='image'
src='https://www.paypal.com/images/x-click-but22.gif'
border='0'
name='submit'  onsubmit='newWindow('600','450','yes',
'paypal','')';>
<input type='hidden' name='add' value='1'>
</form>
```

I am not sure if the onsubmit() should be in the form tag or in the submit button/image tag.

How do I make the above code work?

Also, can the URL parameter be removed from the function?

A: The onsubmit code should be moved from the input to the form. Of course, your "newWindow" function needs to be fixed so it doesn't pass everything as a single parameter nor use reserved words ("window") as parameter names. Your code should read like this:

```
function newWindow(w, h, scroll, windowName, url) {
    var winl = (screen.width - w) / 2;
    var wint = (screen.height - h) / 2;
    winprops =
'height='+h+',width='+w+',top='+wint+',left='+winl+',
scrollbars='+scroll+',resizable';
    win = window.open(url, windowName, winprops);
    if (parseInt(navigator.appVersion, 10) >= 4)
win.focus();
}
```

Then modify your form code as I've said (taking note to not nest the same type of quotes, which you also seem to be doing):

```
<form target="paypal"
action="https://www.paypal.com/cgi-bin/webscr"
method="post" onsubmit="newWindow('600', '450',
'yes', 'paypal', '');">

<input type="image"
src="https://www.paypal.com/images/x-click-but22.gif"
border="0" name="submit">
```

Yes, you can remove the URL parameter if it's not used.

Question 11: Dynamically Reorder a Multiple Select Dropdown

I am trying to write a script that can loop through the contents of a dropdown list and reorder it alphabetically. I can do the looping through, but I don't understand how I can filter it.

It's really easy in server side scripting, but I can't figure it in JS.

Do I loop through the existing dropdown and remove all the elements, then filter, then repopulate? Where can I find an example of reordering an existing dropdown?

A: This code should give you an idea of how to sort a select box. The code has been tested in IE6, but should work in most modern DOM-compliant browsers.

```
<html>
<head>
    <script type="text/javascript">
    <!--

        // sort function - ascending (case-
insensitive)
        function sortFuncAsc(record1, record2) {
            var value1 =
record1.optText.toLowerCase();
            var value2 =
record2.optText.toLowerCase();
            if (value1 > value2) return(1);
            if (value1 < value2) return(-1);
            return(0);
        }

        // sort function - descending (case-
insensitive)
        function sortFuncDesc(record1, record2) {
            var value1 =
record1.optText.toLowerCase();
            var value2 =
record2.optText.toLowerCase();
            if (value1 > value2) return(-1);
            if (value1 < value2) return(1);
            return(0);
```

```
        }

    function sortSelect(selectToSort,
ascendingOrder) {
        if (arguments.length == 1) ascendingOrder
= true;    // default to ascending sort

        // copy options into an array
        var myOptions = [];
        for (var loop=0;
loop<selectToSort.options.length; loop++) {
            myOptions[loop] = {
optText:selectToSort.options[loop].text,
optValue:selectToSort.options[loop].value };
        }

        // sort array
        if (ascendingOrder) {
            myOptions.sort(sortFuncAsc);
        } else {
            myOptions.sort(sortFuncDesc);
        }

        // copy sorted options from array back to
select box
        selectToSort.options.length = 0;
        for (var loop=0; loop<myOptions.length;
loop++) {
            var optObj =
document.createElement('option');
            optObj.text =
myOptions[loop].optText;
            optObj.value =
myOptions[loop].optValue;
            selectToSort.options.add(optObj);
        }
    }
    //-->
    </script>
</head>

<body>
    <form>
        <select name="mySelect">
            <option value="3">Cat</option>
            <option value="4">Dog</option>
            <option value="2">Fish</option>
            <option value="1">Bird</option>
        </select>
```

```
        <br />
        <input type="button"
onclick="sortSelect(this.form['mySelect'], true);"
value="Sort (Asc)">
        <input type="button"
onclick="sortSelect(this.form['mySelect'], false);"
value="Sort (Desc)">
    </form>
</body>
</html>
```

Question 12: Resize the Window with JavaScript

I'm using the following function I found on the Microsoft website to resize the browser window.

```
<script language="JavaScript">
window.onload = maxWindow;

function maxWindow()
{
window.moveTo(0,0);

if (document.all)
{
<!-- I changed the following to constant sizes -->
  top.window.resizeTo(630,700);
//  top.window.resizeTo(screen.availWidth,screen.avai
lHeight);
}
else if (document.layers||document.getElementById)
{
if
(top.window.outerHeight<screen.availHeight||top.windo
w.outerWidth<screen.availWidth)
  {
    top.window.outerHeight = screen.availHeight;
    top.window.outerWidth = screen.availWidth;
  }
}
}
```

It works fine with one htm file. However, with another file that works well without this function, I'm getting the following security warning:

"To help protect your security, Internet Explorer had restricted from showing active content that could access your computer. Click here for options..."

What is the cause of this problem?

A: You are running the HTML page locally and not through a web server. If you have Windows XP Pro with IIS installed, or any other web server, run the page through the server and you shouldn't have that message show up.

Question 13: IE: Element.setAttribute Not Working

I'm working on an application that needs to use the DOM to dynamically edit attributes for elements. But for some reason Internet Explorer doesn't recognize the command setAttribute(attribute, value):

```
document.getElementById("mapimage").innerHTML =
data[map][5];
var usemap = "#" + data[map][0];
document.getElementById("trans").setAttribute("usemap
", usemap);
```

On the first line, I'm populating the imagemap with the data I got from the server. Line 2 makes the imagemap reference and line 3 should set the new imagemap. But on testing, the attribute stays the same. The code works great in Firefox. Is there anyway to make it work in Internet Explorer as well?

A: Welcome to the world of IE and its non-standard calls. You should add a third parameter, which will do nothing in compliant browsers, but it will tell IE to ignore any case issues:

```
setAttribute('usemap', usemap, 0);
```

Read here for more:
http://msdn.microsoft.com/library/default.asp?url=/workshop/author/dhtml/reference/methods/setattribute.asp

Question 14:
document.Date.TodayDate.value

I tried to write a simple piece of code that puts the current date into a textboxfield. The current date should be written like this: 20062404

This is what I have so far:

```
<form name="Date">
<input size=20 maxlength=75 type='text'
name='TodayDate' value=""></form>
<script language="JavaScript" type="text/JavaScript">
var date = new Date();
var d  = date.getDate();
var day = (d < 10) ? '0' + d : d;
var m = date.getMonth() + 1;
var month = (m < 10) ? '0' + m : m;
var yy = date.getYear();
var year = (yy < 1000) ? yy + 1900 : yy;
document.Date.TodayDate.value.(year + month + day);
</script>
```

The following statement doesn't work either:

```
document.Date.TodayDate.value=(year + month + day);
```

The html page this code has to work on is generated by a Webfocus report. The actual html is:

```
<input size=20 maxlength=75 type='text'
name='TodayDate' value="">
```

I don't have anything but the textbox in my html. If I use [form] and [/form], then my html will not function anymore. How do I get the current date into the textbox?

A: The following line is invalid and will not work:

```
document.Date.TodayDate.value.(year + month + day);
```

Use a more direct method to put the value into the box by adding an ID tag to the field:

```
<input size=20 maxlength=75 type='text'
name='TodayDate' id='TodayDate' value="">
```

Then use this DOM method to add the value:

```
document.getElementById('TodayDate').value=(year +
month + day);
```

If you are in an IE-only shop, you may be able to use document.all to get around specifying the name of the form in order to reach the form element. But the DOM method above is the best way to go if it works for you.

Question 15: Center a div for onClick Pop-up Style Event

The following script is supposed to load an enlarged image once the small image is clicked.

```
<script language="JavaScript">

var ie=document.all
var ns6=document.getElementById&&!document.all

function ietruebody(){
return (document.compatMode!="BackCompat")?
document.documentElement : document.body
}

function enlarge(which, e, position, imgwidth,
imgheight){
if (ie||ns6){
crossobj=document.getElementById?
document.getElementById("showimage") :
document.all.showimage
if (position=="center"){
pgyoffset=ns6? parseInt(pageYOffset) :
parseInt(ietruebody().scrollTop)
horzpos=ns6? pageXOffset+window.innerWidth/2-
imgwidth/2 :
ietruebody().scrollLeft+ietruebody().clientWidth/2-
imgwidth/2
```

```
vertpos=ns6? pgyoffset+window.innerHeight/2-
imgheight/2 : pgyoffset+ietruebody().clientHeight/2-
imgheight/2
if (window.opera && window.innerHeight) //compensate
for Opera toolbar
vertpos=pgyoffset+window.innerHeight/2-imgheight/2
vertpos=Math.max(pgyoffset, vertpos)
}
else{
var horzpos=ns6? pageXOffset+e.clientX :
ietruebody().scrollLeft+event.clientX
var vertpos=ns6? pageYOffset+e.clientY :
ietruebody().scrollTop+event.clientY
}
crossobj.style.left=horzpos+"px"
crossobj.style.top=vertpos+"px"

crossobj.innerHTML='<div align="right"
id="dragbar"><span id="closetext"
onClick="closepreview()">Close X</span></div><img
src="'+which+'">'
crossobj.style.visibility="visible"
return false
}
else //if NOT IE 4+ or NS 6+, simply display image in
full browser window
return true
}

function closepreview(){
crossobj.style.visibility="hidden"
}

function drag_drop(e){
if (ie&&dragapproved){
crossobj.style.left=tempx+event.clientX-offsetx+"px"
crossobj.style.top=tempy+event.clientY-offsety+"px"
}
else if (ns6&&dragapproved){
crossobj.style.left=tempx+e.clientX-offsetx+"px"
crossobj.style.top=tempy+e.clientY-offsety+"px"
}
return false
}

function initializedrag(e){
if
(ie&&event.srcElement.id=="dragbar"||ns6&&e.target.id
=="dragbar"){
```

```
offsetx=ie? event.clientX : e.clientX
offsety=ie? event.clientY : e.clientY

tempx=parseInt(crossobj.style.left)
tempy=parseInt(crossobj.style.top)

dragapproved=true
document.onmousemove=drag_drop
}
}

document.onmousedown=initializedrag
document.onmouseup=new Function("dragapproved=false")
```

```
<div id="showimage"></div>
<script language="JavaScript"><!--
document.write('<?php echo '<a href="'. DIR_WS_IMAGES
. $product_info['products_image'].'" onClick="return
enlarge(\\\''. DIR_WS_IMAGES .
$product_info['products_image'].'\\\',event,\\\'cente
r\\\','.$size[0].','.$size[1].')" >' .
tep_image(DIR_WS_IMAGES .
$product_info['products_image'],
$product_info['products_name'], SMALL_IMAGE_WIDTH,
SMALL_IMAGE_HEIGHT, 'hspace="5" vspace="5"') . '<br>'
. TEXT_CLICK_TO_ENLARGE .'</a>'; ?>');
```

The new image is displayed in the center of the screen. It can be dragged and closed, but only in IE. In Firefox and other browsers, however, the new image is loaded directly over the small image, pushing it down the page.

The code works in IE, but how do I make it work in other popular browsers such as Firefox, Opera, and Netscape?

A: Use absolute positioning for the whole thing. Changing the dimensions of the window causes issues with things moving around. Using absolute positioning keeps everything c entered.

Your code does not show a setting for absolute positioning so it is probably defaulting to relative positioning.

Change your div to this and try it:

```
<div id="showimage" style="position:
absolute;"></div>
```

You are bound to run into centering problems in different browsers since the methods of retrieving the screen dimensions vary quite a bit. Some methods work in some browsers and some in others. To make it worse, a method that works in more than one browser may return the values differently. For instance, innerHeight returns the height of the content area in Firefox but it does not take into account if a horizontal scrollbar is there so your effective content area is less than the number returned depending on how t all the scrollbar is. I see you set to compensate for a toolbar in Opera but check your dimensions within Firefox.

When your div is using relative positioning, it will displace other objects on the page. When set to absolute, it will float right over top of the page and any other elements; unless, of course, they are also set to absolute, then you get into layering.

Question 16: Directly Parse an ical Calendar File

I am trying to find a way to parse event lists in the ical /vcalendar format into a much simpler event array in JavaScript. (I throw away much of the calendar information, keeping only the date and the summary.)

If I first open the ical file and add a var cal=" to the beginning, a " to the end, and either remove all line endings or add a \ at the end of each, I can do it. The resulting file is then treated as an ordinary external .js file and cal is simply a string that can be parsed for the data I want to be part of the JavaScript event array.

Is it possible to take the raw ical file and have it read as either an array or a string without the initial editing in of the var cal=" \"stuff? How?

A: Reading from text files is possible in IE using a proprietary ActiveX control, which doesn't work in any other browser, and possibly in Firefox or other browsers using some sort of Java IO routines.

Your best bet is to keep editing the files, or parse them out server-side to deliver the correct "JS" files to the client.

Question 17: Error with ClearText(this) Function

I have 2 input types of text with a value that when clicked, the value (set text) clears. I have to build myASP page up as a string.

```
LPRSearchHead1 = "<script language=""JavaScript""
type=""text/javascript"">" & VBCRLF
LPRSearchHead1 = LPRSearchHead1 & "function
clearText(thefield) {" & VBCRLF
LPRSearchHead1 = LPRSearchHead1 & "if
(thefield.defaultValue = thefield.value){" & VBCRLF
LPRSearchHead1 = LPRSearchHead1 & "thefield.value =
""" & VBCRLF
LPRSearchHead1 = LPRSearchHead1 & "    }" & VBCRLF
LPRSearchHead1 = LPRSearchHead1 & "else {" & VBCRLF
LPRSearchHead1 = LPRSearchHead1 & "thefield.value =
thefield.defaultValue" & VBCRLF
LPRSearchHead1 = LPRSearchHead1 & "}" & VBCRLF
LPRSearchHead1 = LPRSearchHead1 & "}</script>" &
VBCRLF
```

There are <FORM> and </FORM> tags and the text box is as follows:

```
LPRSearchBody = LPRSearchBody & "<td
width=""60%""><strong><input type=""text"" id=""fp1""
name=""SchTradingName"" size=""35"" value=""Enter
Trading Name"" onClick=""clearText(this) ""
/></strong></td>"
```

However, I get the following error message: "Object expected"

How do I correct this error?

A: Try the following:

```
>LPRSearchHead1 = LPRSearchHead1 & "thefield.value =
""" & VBCRLF
LPRSearchHead1 = LPRSearchHead1 & "thefield.value =
""""" & VBCRLF
```

Question 18: Window.open Not Working in Firefox

I have the following function, which works in IE but not in Firefox. It comes with a 404 error.

```
<script language='javascript'>
    var workObj
      function
domainsearch(strFname,strSearchName,idx)
      {    window.open("domainkeysearch.asp?search="
& strSearchName & "&retObj=" & strFname &
"&usexsl=xsl/oa_rawlist.xsl&idx=" &
idx,"NEW","scrollbars=yes,width=400,height=400,left=1
35,top=120")
      }
</script>
```

How do I correct the error?

A: Concatenate the string (window.open) with +'s instead of &'s.

Question 19: onChange Not Working

I have onChange on a select drop down list. The following code worked on an old server but not on the server I recently set up:

```
<select name="changeClient"
onChange="location.href=(form.changeClient.options[fo
rm.changeClient.selectedIndex].value)">
```

I have a button code that is not working either:

```
<input type="submit" name="submit" value="Send
Message" onClick="sendmsg.asp?id=1">
```

How do I make it work?

A: The following statement is an invalid JavaScript:

```
onClick="sendmsg.asp?id=1"
```

```
"sendmsg.asp?id=1" is simply a URL. onClick handlers
should take valid script.
```

If you want the select element to simply change the URL, then use this:

```
<select name="changeClient" onchange="location.href =
this.value;">
```

If you want the submit button to submit to the URL you previously had in the onClick handler, you should remove the onClick from the button and move the content to the form's action:

```
<form action="sendmsg.asp">
    <input type="submit" name="mySubmit" value="Send
Message">
</form>
```

Question 20: Match textarea Size to Window

I want to create a child window for editing the content of the parent, with a big textarea that will fill as much area of the window as possible (except for a little spot for Apply and Reset buttons). The problem is that window sizes are in pixels, but textarea sizes are in rows and cols. The textarea properties clientHeight and clientWidth are in pixels, but appear to be just informational (read-only). The only way I can think of to get the size right is to create the window and the textarea with some starting size that is a guess, and then have a loop where I test clientHeight and clientWidth against the window size and change rows and/or cols accordingly, over and over, until it fits. That seems cheesy.

I will be specifying my textarea's font size in CSS, but I like using "pt" for font sizes, and I suspect that the ratio between points, pixels, and textarea rows/cols varies bybrowser. Even if I use "px" instead, that would only help define the height. The width of a character in the fixed-spaced font of the browser would still be an unknown.

Is there a better way to work around this?

A: While you can specify an initial size for your textarea in row & cols for those with no CSS support, you can simply override these for those who do:

```
<textarea rows="5" cols="5"
style="width:600px;height:300px;"></textarea>
```

Question 21: Find Object from String

I have a form, which is sent to the server using AJAX, and it has some server-side validating. When an error occurs, I will alert the user and put focus on the field that gives the error. I send back the string (responsetext) from server then use split in JavaScript to set it up. After the split, I have, say, response[0] with the name of the object that did not pass the server test (e.g., wrong password and the name of the password field is passw, response[0]=passw).

What do I do to set the focus on passw?

A: Use the following:

```
document.forms['your form name
here'].elements['passw'].focus();
```

Question 22: Retrieve HTML Code

I'm working on a site with 3 frames (master, demoframe, and sourceframe). When a user clicks on a link in the navbar (master), an html file is opened in demoframe. What I need to do now is create a function I can call from either master or sourceframe to read the html code from the page I just opened in demoframe into a string (parsing it from there is not the issue, just need to retrieve the html code).

Bandwidth on my server is at a minimum right now, so I need to do this *without* generating another request for the .html file from my server (i.e., all handling and manipulation must be client-side).

How do I make this happen? Is there a DOM object out of which I can read a page's source code?

A: Assuming you know how to access the frame, call the following and it should give you the output of the page:

```
var str =
document.getElementsByTagName("html")[0].innerHTML;
alert(str);
```

This should return all the code for the page (minus the <html> tags). If you want to see the <html> tags then you can use outerHTML, but that is for IE only, I believe.

Question 23: Put Value in href Address

With the following code:

```
<a id="my_link"
href="details_page.htm?Page_point=X">Go to details
page</a>
```

```
<html>
<head>
<title>Test Document</title>
<meta http-equiv="Content-Type" content="text/html;
charset=iso-8859-1">

</head>

<body>
<form id="js_test">
  <input type="hidden" id="point">
  <a id="my_link"
href="details_page.htm?Page_point=hidden field
value">Go to details page</a>

</form>
</body>
</html>
```

Is there a way to put the current value of a hidden field in this link (where X is) when user clicks on the link?

A: Try the following code:

```
<html>
<head>
<title>Test Document</title>
<meta http-equiv="Content-Type" content="text/html;
charset=iso-8859-1">
<script type="text/javascript">

function setValue(obj) {
    var x = document.getElementById("point").value;
```

```
    obj.href = "details_page.htm?Page_point=" + x;
    return true
}
</script>
</head>

<body>
<form id="js_test">
   <input type="hidden" id="point">
   <a id="my_link" href="details_page.htm"
onclick="setValue(this)">Go to details page</a>

</form>
</body>
</html>
```

-kaht

To be brief, use the following:

```
<form id="js_test">
   <input type="hidden" id="point">
   <a href="details_page.htm" onclick="this.href +=
'?Page_point=' + document.js_test.point.value; return
true;">Go to details page</a>

</form>
```

You may also want to add a semi-colon ";" after both "return true;" and "onClick="setValue(this);". Although this may not be *necessary*, it may solve some future browser issues before they start and makes the syntax a little cleaner.

It would be very tempting to try using an onMouseOver="setValue(this);" in place of onClick="...;", although this, too, is probably unnecessary (by syntax, the JavaScript in onClick="...;" *should* be processed before the HTML gets to process the href), but to be safe, give the browser a couple of extra tenths of a second to prep the href attribute *before* the user clicks on the link.

Question 24: Firefox get Value from Another Frame

I have the following (simplified) HTML.

```
<!DOCTYPE HTML PUBLIC "-//W3C//DTD HTML 4.01
Frameset//EN">
<html>
<head>

<script language="JavaScript" type="text/javascript">

</script>
</head>

<frameset rows="15%,85%">

<frame name="fraTopNav" src="about:blank">

<frameset cols="17%,83%">

<frameset rows="87%,13%">

<frame name="fraSideNav"
src="/MattTest.nsf/SideNav?OpenPage">

<frame name="fraFamilyID"
src="/MattTest.nsf/FamilyID?OpenForm"
id="fraFamilyID">
</frameset>

<frameset rows="32%,44%">

<frame name="fraNewPerson" src="about:blank">

<frame name="fraExistingPeople" src="about:blank">
</frameset>
</frameset>
</frameset>
</html>
```

In the frame fraNewPerson I have a form and then the following code runs on a button click event:

```
if (confirm("Are you sure you wish to submit?"))
{
    top.fraFamilyID._FamilyID.TEMPFamilyID.value =
"TEST";
    window.document.forms[0].submit()
}
```

It works fine in IE and Opera but in Firefox and Netscape it fails. When I try to set the value of the textbox that is on the other frame, I get the following error message:

```
top.fraFamilyID._FamilyID has no properties
```

How do I correct this error?

A: The following should work for all browsers:

```
>top.fraFamilyID._FamilyID.TEMPFamilyID.value =
"TEST";
top.fraFamilyID.document._FamilyID.TEMPFamilyID.value
= "TEST";
```

Question 25: Disabled textarea

I have a multi-line textbox, which I have disabled so users can only view the text, not edit it. How can I enable the scrollbar in case there is more text than what fits in the area?

A: Make it read-only. And if eventually you do not want to submit it, turn it to disabled at submit time. Remember when using the disabled property, any input fields with disabled set will NOT submit their values when the form submits so you would not be able to read those values in the next page.

In some cases that would not matter to you because if the field was disabled, they could not change the option. The value may not be needed but if, for instance, you read the form values in an ASP page you would have to test if the value came in NULL so your script does not hang up furtherdown the line.

If you set readOnly within the HTML of the textarea then case is not important, but if you try to toggle the readOnly property from JavaScript then it must be readOnly with the capital O. You could spend a lot of time trying to figure out why it is not working otherwise.

Question 26: List Box to hide/display DIV

I am having problems with the following code:

```
<style type="text/css"> #a1, #a2, #a3, #a4, #a5 {
DISPLAY: none; } </style>

<script type="text/javascript">
 function Toggle(determine) {
document.getElementById("a1").style.display = "none";
document.getElementById("a2").style.display = "none";
document.getElementById("a3").style.display = "none";
document.getElementById("a4").style.display = "none";
document.getElementById("a5").style.display =
"none";
document.getElementById(determine).style.display =
"block";
}
</script>

<select size="1" name="determine"
onChange="Toggle(document.determine.getElementById.va
lue);">
<option value="a1">This</option>
<option value="a2">That</option>
<option value="a3">Here</option>
<option value="a4">There</option>
<option value="a5">Some</option>
</select>

<div id="a1">this</div>
<div id="a2">that</div>
<div id="a3">here</div>
<div id="a4">there</div>
<div id="a5">some</div>
```

What is wrong with the code?

A: You need to edit the following statement to correct the code.

```
<select size="1" name="determine"
onChange="Toggle(this.value);">
```

Question 27: Dynamically Created Text Boxes

I'm using AJAX to validate data entered by a user into a textbox, AJAX that data, and create a new textbox so the user can enter more data to be validated.

```
<input type=text name='cd0'
onblur='populateSections(document.forms[\"adminForm\"
], this.value, \"user\");'>
<input type=text name='cd1'
onblur='populateSections(document.forms[\"adminForm\"
], this.value, \"user\");'>
<input type=text name='cdn'
onblur='populateSections(document.forms[\"adminForm\"
], this.value, \"user\");'>
```

In the following function, I want to be able to read in an 'n' number of values from textboxes named 'cd1' through 'cdn'.

```
x=0;
while (document.myFormName.cdx)
{
   readData = document.myFormName.cdx.value;
   //Do some AJAX stuff with the readData (rebuild the
textboxes and add a new empty textbox with
name="cdx+1"
   x++;   //Go around again and read the next textbox
value if there is one
}
```

How do I get JavaScript to read back the values from an unknown number of textboxes?

A: You need to use the forms and elements collections. You'll have a lot fewer problems when you use them consistently.

```
var x = 0;
var readData;
while (document.forms["formName"].elements["cd" + x])
```

```
{
   readData =
document.forms["formName"].elements["cd" + x].value;
   //do stuff
   x++;
}
```

Question 28: Textbox Highlight "Text" and "Replace"

I'm trying to make a very basic text editor that has image buttons for formatting the text. I use the following code:

```
Sub btnBold_Click (Sender as Object, e as
ImageClickEventArgs)
    If Session("boldText") = "boldOff" then
        Dim textForBold As String = txtContent.text
        Dim textBoldStart As String = textForBold +
"[&#91;]b]"
        txtContent.text = textBoldStart
        lblStatus.Text = "Text Entry is Bold. (click
on Bold Text button again to end Bold Text)"
        Session("boldText") = "boldOn"
    Else
        Dim textForBold As String = txtContent.text
        Dim textBoldEnd As String = textForBold +
"[&#91;]/b]"
        txtContent.text = textBoldEnd
        lblStatus.Text = "Text Entry is Normal."
        Session("boldText") = "boldOff"
    End If
End Sub
```

For example, in the textbox containing the following text: "The dog ran after the ball", if I select and highlight "dog ran after", then press the bold image button I created, it will replace the text in the following way:

The [b]dog ran after[/b] the ball.

How do I write the code so that the cursor will highlight text in the textbox and when the bold image button is pressed, it will automatically make the highlighted text bold by putting the selected text between [b] and [/b]?

A: The following code works in IE6 and FF1.5:

```
<script type="text/javascript">
function blah() {
    var ta = document.getElementById("test");
    if (document.selection) {
        str = document.selection.createRange().text
        document.selection.createRange().text = "[b]" +
str + "[/b]";
        return true;
    }
    else if (ta.selectionStart) {
        var startPos = ta.selectionStart;
        var endPos = ta.selectionEnd;
        var str = ta.value.substring(startPos, endPos);
        ta.value = ta.value.substring(0, startPos) +
"[b]" + str + "[/b]" + ta.value.substring(endPos,
ta.value.length);
        return true;
    }
    else {
        return false;
    }
}
</script>
<input type="button" value="Bold" onclick="blah()" />
<br />
<textarea id="test" style="height:150px">
This is a test to see if the bold tags will work.
</textarea>
```

You may also take a look at one of these two products:

- TinyMCE, or
- FCKEdit

Both are FREE rich-text editors for multiple browsers that do not rely on the HTML textarea object, and you could either switch to using them, or look into their code to see how they achieve this.

You cannot alter the properties of text with the HTML textarea so you cannot set text to bold, italic, different colors, etc. The only control for this is setting the properties on the textarea object itself and it applies to all of the text within that box.

You can make one yourself by creating a virtual textarea, or in other words an area that by design looks like a textarea field but is actually not and therefore does not have the limitations of one.

It can be a bit cumbersome to write one yourself, especially if you want to support other browsers. You have to deal with key trapping and text selection events that work differently in different browsers.

Question 29: Confirm Before Second Function

I'm trying to impose a "confirm" before executing the second function with the following code:

```
onClick='return confirm('Are you sure you want to
delete this
application?');funcDeleteApplication();'><img
src='images/btnDel.gif' /></a>"
```

What is the proper syntax for this?

A: Try one of the following:

```
onclick='if confirm("Are you sure you want to delete
this application?") funcDeleteApplication();'>

onClick='if (confirm('Are you sure you want to delete
this application?')) {funcDeleteApplication();}'><img
src='images/btnDel.gif' /></a>"
```

Question 30: Hide/Show Radio Buttons

The following code works when I refresh the page before selecting a different option in the drop down. If I select a different option without refreshing the page, it does not show me any Radio Buttons.

```
<html>
<head>
<meta http-equiv="Content-Type" content="text/html;
charset=windows-1252">
<meta name="GENERATOR" content="Microsoft FrontPage
4.0">
<meta name="ProgId"
content="FrontPage.Editor.Document">
<title>New Page 1</title>
<script type="text/javascript">
```

```
function funcCalc(s)
{
if(s == 1)
{
obj = document.getElementById('group2').style;
(obj.display == 'none')? obj.display = 'block' :
obj.display = 'none';
if
(document.getElementById('group3').style.visibility="
visible")
document.getElementById('group3').style.visibility="h
idden"
if
(document.getElementById('group5').style.visibility="
visible")
document.getElementById('group5').style.visibility="h
idden"
}

if(s == 2)
{
obj = document.getElementById('group3').style;
(obj.display == 'none')? obj.display = 'block' :
obj.display = 'none';
if
(document.getElementById('group2').style.visibility="
visible")
document.getElementById('group2').style.visibility="h
idden"
if
(document.getElementById('group5').style.visibility="
visible")
document.getElementById('group5').style.visibility="h
idden"
}

if(s == 3)
{
obj = document.getElementById('group5').style;
(obj.display == 'none')? obj.display = 'block' :
obj.display = 'none';
if
(document.getElementById('group2').style.visibility="
visible")
document.getElementById('group2').style.visibility="h
idden"
if
(document.getElementById('group3').style.visibility="
visible")
```

```
document.getElementById('group3').style.visibility="h
idden"
}
}
</script>
</head>

<body>

<form id="form1" name="form1" method="post"
action="">
Calculations:
<SELECT NAME="First"
onChange="funcCalc(this.selectedIndex)" size ="1"
style="font-size: 8pt; font-family:Arial
color:000080; font-weight:bold">
<OPTION VALUE="N/A">--- Does application use
calculations ?--
<OPTION VALUE="Yes"> Yes
<OPTION VALUE="No"> No
<OPTIOn VALUE="Not Sure"> Not Sure
</SELECT>
<br>
  <p id="group2" style="display: none;">
    <label>
    <input type="radio" name="RadioGroup2"
value="radio" />
Radio99</label>
    <br />
    <label>
    <input type="radio" name="RadioGroup2"
value="radio" />
Radio99</label>

    <br />

<p id="group3" style="display: none;">
    <label>
    <input type="radio" name="RadioGroup3"
value="radio" />
Radio100</label>
    <br />
    <label>
    <input type="radio" name="RadioGroup3"
value="radio" />
Radio100</label>

    <br />

<p id="group5" style="display: none;">
```

```
    <label>
    <input type="radio" name="RadioGroup5"
value="radio" />
Radio102</label>
    <br />
    <label>
    <input type="radio" name="RadioGroup5"
value="radio" />
Radio102</label>

    <br />

</p>
</form>

</body>

</html>
```

I want to show a different set of radio buttons each time the user selects a different option in the drop down. For example, I want to show the Radio Buttons associated with "Yes" when it is selected from the drop down. But if I switch the option to "No", it should take away the Radio Buttons for "Yes" and only show the Radio Buttons for "No". How do I make this happen?

Also, if I have a Submit Button at the end of the code, it only shows if I select the last option in the drop down. How do I make it show even if the last option is not selected?

A: Get rid of the inner if statements. You're setting the visibility to hidden, so even if you set the display to block, the elements are still hidden. You never change any elements to visible then. Change to the following and see what happens.

```
function funcCalc(s)
{
var obj;
if(s == 1)
   {
   obj = document.getElementById('group2').style;
   (obj.display == 'none')? obj.display = 'block' :
obj.display = 'none';

   document.getElementById('group3').style.display =
'none';
```

```
    document.getElementById('group5').style.display =
'none';
    }

if(s == 2)
   {
   obj = document.getElementById('group3').style;
   (obj.display == 'none')? obj.display = 'block' :
obj.display = 'none';

   document.getElementById('group2').style.display =
'none';
   document.getElementById('group5').style.display =
'none';
    }

if(s == 3)
   {
   obj = document.getElementById('group5').style;
   (obj.display == 'none')? obj.display = 'block' :
obj.display = 'none';
   document.getElementById('group2').style.display =
'none';
   document.getElementById('group3').style.display =
'none';
    }
}
```

As for the Submit button, I guess you have it inside the <p> tag that contains the last set of radio buttons. Take it out of those tags and it should display fine.

Question 31: Editable div

I have created a small table using <div>'s with the following
HTML code and I would like to give the user the abilty to
edit/add text.

```
<script src="editDiv.js"
type="text/javascript"></script>

<div class="nameBox" id="fName"
onclick="edit(this)"></div>
<div class="addBox" id="add"
onclick="edit(this)"></div>
```

The JavaScript is where I have issues. I would like my editDiv.js
file to: a) generate a pop-up with a text field, and b) once the user
clicks "OK" the content of the textbox is placed in the appropriate
<div> (using innerHTML). Since the content editable attribute
is not entirely "cross-browser", is there any alternative approach?

A: Try the following code:

```
<script>
function edit(inObj){
  newTxt = document.getElementById("newText").value
  if (document.all){
    inObj.innerHTML = newTxt
  }
  else{

    inObj.childNodes(0).textNode = newTxt
  }
}
</script>

<div class="nameBox" id="fName"
onclick="edit(this)"></div>
<div class="addBox" id="add"
onclick="edit(this)"></div>

<textarea id='newText'></textarea>
```

Question 32: & in location.href

This code works on my site:

```
document.location.href = "mailto:?subject=You'll like
this page on HandicappedPets.com&body=It's at: "+
window.document.location.href
```

But when I get to this page:
http://www.handicappedpets.com/gallery/index.php?category_i
d=&parent_id=0&photo_id=8&countdisplay=&start=
0,

it gets processed as:
http://www.handicappedpets.com/gallery/index.php?category_i
d=

I assume the & sign in the address is bothering it. How do I get
around this?

A: Escape the string by using the following code:

```
document.location.href = "mailto:?subject=You'll like
this page on HandicappedPets.com&body=It's at: " +
escape(window.document.location.href);
```

Question 33: Populate a Text Box With a Dropdown Value

I've tried several methods mentioned on this subject but can't get any of them to work. Below is my latest attempt:

```
<form name="MyForm" action="MyInvoice.htm"
method="post">
    Amount:
    <input type="Text" name="Amount" size="10"
value="55">
    <br>
    Type:
    <select name="ProductType">
        <option value="33"
onchange="FillAmount();">Product A</option>
        <option value="55"
onchange="FillAmount();">Product B</option>
    </select>
    <input type="Submit" value="Print">
</form>

<script type="text/javascript" language="JavaScript">
    function FillAmount()
    {
        MyForm.Amount.value =
MyForm.ProductType.options[MyForm.ProductType.selecte
dIndex].value;
    }
</script>
```

How do I populate a text box with a dropdown value?

A: Try the following:

```
<form name="MyForm" action="MyInvoice.htm"
method="post">
    Amount:
    <input type="Text" name="Amount" size="10"
value="33" />
    <br>
    Type:
    <select name="ProductType"
onchange="FillAmount() ">
```

```
            <option value="33">Product A</option>
            <option value="55">Product B</option>
    </select>
    <input type="Submit" value="Print" />
</form>

<script type="text/javascript" language="JavaScript">
    function FillAmount()
    {
        document.forms["MyForm"].elements["Amount"].v
alue =
document.forms["MyForm"].elements["ProductType"].opti
ons[document.forms["MyForm"].elements["ProductType"].
selectedIndex].value;
    }
</script>
```

Question 34: User to Select a Specific Day

I have three dropdowns which represent a date — one for the date, one for the month, and one for the year. The problem is that I need to force people to select a Friday.

I create a date object from these 3 fields and then I use getDay() to find out which day of the week the user has selected.

This is where I'm getting stuck: if the user selects 23/03/2006 (a Thursday), I need the date dropdown to automatically change to 24 (the nearest Friday). Is there a way to do this?

A: This isn't quite your answer, but you can use it to get there:

```
var today = new Date();
 var dayOfWeek = today.getDay(); //returns 0 - 6
 while(dayOfWeek != 5) //5 is Friday
 {
  today.setDate(today.getDate() + 1);
  dayOfWeek = today.getDay();
 }
```

//at this point, "today" equals the next Friday.

You can use a variation of this code to set the date to t he values in the dropdown lists and then cycle upward from there until the dayOfWeek is equal to 5.

Question 35: Equivalent of VB's Right$() function

I have a filename, let's say, of 'MyFile.xls'. I want to strip off the filename and preserve it, so I would have two variables:

```
string1 = 'MyFile'
string2 = '.xls'
```

I will append a timestamp to string1 :
string1 = string1 + timestamp

Then I want to append string2 back onto string1:
string1 = string1 + string2

How do I write the code?

A: You'll want to use the lastIndexOf method combined with the substr or substring method:

```
<script type="text/javascript">

function blah(str) {
    var pos = str.lastIndexOf(".");
    if (pos != -1) {
        var string1 = str.substr(0, pos);
        var string2 = str.substr(pos, str.length -
pos);
        var timestamp = "03/21/2006";
        string1 = string1 + timestamp;
        alert(string1 + string2);
    }
    else {
        alert("decimal could not be found");
    }
}

</script>
<input type="text" id="txt" />
<input type="button" value="Click me"
onclick="blah(document.getElementById('txt').value)"
/>
```

Question 36: GUI – Interface

Is it true that Win XP with service pack 2 prevents the opening of a full screen window?

Is it possible to have true full screen by moving the close/minimize bar off the screen?

Is there a better way of creating a desktop App feel to an online GUI if you can get the client to add the websites to the trusted sites list?

A: Your questions are both based upon the assumption that you're talking about Internet Explorer. Other browsers may not be so restrictive. WRT to IE, you could use an HTA (HTML Application) to become "trusted" and gain more privileges.

Question 37: Leave Frameset in Browser

I am trying to use a window.open script in a frameset to open a new window outside the frameset, but leave the frameset running in the browser as well. I am building a sort of simple help system for a site prototype, and I am using the right frame to hold help links that will pop up.

I have seen a script where you can add to the head of a new document to break the frameset, but it is not what I need. What is the appropriate script to use?

A: If all you want to do is open a pop-up window, you can use a regular pop-up window script for that—even if you are running in a frameset:

```
var winHandle =
window.open('http://www.google.co.uk/', '', '');
```

Question 38: Window self.close Problem

I am using the following code to open a new window when someone clicks on the link, but I would like to close the parent window after the click.

```
<a href="javascript:void(null)"
onClick="makeNewWindow0091();javascript:self.close()"
>Link</a>
```

The new window is opened when the user has clicked on the link, but a pop-up box appears and asks the user if they really want to close the window. How can I stop the pop-up box and close the window automatically?

A: Try this:

```
<a href="javascript:void(null);"
onclick="makeNewWindow0091(); this.opener=self;
self.close();">Link</a>
```

Question 39: Set Selected Option

How can I tell a select to make a particular option selected?

A: Try either of the following:

```
document.forms["formName"].elements["selectBoxName"].
selectedIndex = x
```

-or-

```
document.forms["formName"].elements["selectBoxName"].
value = "whatever value you want to set it to"
```

Question 40: Change document.body.offsetWidth

I'm trying to get the width of the screen and set my CSS columns to be of a certain width so that they fit the screen perfectly.

Apparently, the function picks up my resolution (1280x1024), which does not include the scrollbar on the right. This makes my columns align improperly because it is not of the right size when the page is fully loaded.

Here's my JavaScript code:

```
function fixWidth()
{
    var maincontent, header, changeto;
    changeto =
document.getElementById("box").offsetWidth - 400; //
Set the width of the columns, left column = 200px,
right column =  200px
    maincontent =
document.getElementById("maincontent"); // Get center
column
    header = document.getElementById("header"); //
Get top column
    maincontent.style.width = changeto + "px"; // Set
center column's width
    header.style.width = changeto + "px"; // Set top
column's width
}
```

When the page is loaded, the offsetWidth is 1264 (16 pixels for the scroll bar in Firefox, 20 for IE). How I can fix this?

A: The function should only be called when the page is fully loaded, then put the call in the BODY tag's ONLOAD event.

You may also use clientWidth instead of offsetWidth.

Question 41: Loop Not Detecting Data

I am trying to create a function so that if data in a table row is duplicated (e.g., 4), then the function will display an alert indicating that the function has detected a row of data which is exactly the same.

Here is the code:

```
<script language="javascript">

function test()
{
VV = document.getElementsByTagName('td');

for(A = 0;A < VV.length;A++)
{

VV[A].innerHTML = '45'
VV[A].setAttribute('onClick',"this.innerHTML = '4'")

}

}

function grr()
{
Y = new Array();
TY = 0;
XX = document.getElementsByTagName('td');
NN = document.getElementsByTagName('td');
for(A = 0;A < XX.length;A++)
{
    Y[A] = XX[A].innerHTML;
    }
alert(Y.length)
for(BB = 8 * TY;BB < Y.length;BB = BB + 8)
{
alert(TY)

//Problem Area
if('4'==Y[BB].innerHTML && '4'==Y[BB+1].innerHTML &&
'4'==Y[BB+2].innerHTML  && '4'==Y[BB+3].innerHTML &&
'4'==Y[BB+4].innerHTML && '4'==Y[BB+5].innerHTML &&
'4'==Y[BB+6].innerHTML  && '4'==Y[BB+7].innerHTML)
{
```

```
        alert('a row of fours have been detected');
}
TY++
}
}
window.onload = test;
</script>
<table cellspacing=0 width=670 border=1>
<td> </td><td> </td><td> </td><td> </
td><td> </td><td> </td><td> </td><td>&nbs
p</td><tr>
<td> </td><td> </td><td> </td><td> </
td><td> </td><td> </td><td> </td><td>&nbs
p</td><tr>
<td> </td><td> </td><td> </td><td> </
td><td> </td><td> </td><td> </td><td>&nbs
p</td><tr>
<td> </td><td> </td><td> </td><td> </
td><td> </td><td> </td><td> </td><td>&nbs
p</td><tr>
</table>
<input type="button" onClick=grr()>
```

However, for some reason, the function does not detect the
correct data in a row. I checked the JavaScript console and it has
not displayed any errors. How can I make the function detect the
data?

A: Try the following:

```
function grr(){
    Y = new Array();
    TY = 0;
    XX = document.getElementsByTagName('td');
    NN = document.getElementsByTagName('td');
    for(A = 0;A < XX.length;A++){
        Y[A] = XX[A].innerHTML;
    }
    alert(Y.length)
    for(BB = 8 * TY;BB < Y.length;BB = BB + 8){
        alert(BB)
        //alert(Y)
        //Problem Area
        if('4'==Y[BB] && '4'==Y[BB+1] &&
'4'==Y[BB+2]   && '4'==Y[BB+3] && '4'==Y[BB+4] &&
'4'==Y[BB+5] && '4'==Y[BB+6]   && '4'==Y[BB+7])
```

```
        {
            alert('a row of fours have been
detected');
        }
        TY++
    }
}
```

I removed the ".innerHTML" from the if statements since you are comparing the values to an array. It worked in Firefox when all 8 values in the row = '4'.

Question 42: "scrollTo" is Not Working in IE6 or Opera

I am trying to use window.scrollTo(x, y) after a page has finished loading. The code works fine in Netscape/Mozilla, but fails in Opera/IE6 and possibly other versions of IE. I was obtaining the x/y coordinates dynamically, but since it was not working I have them hard-coded, for now. My code is:

```
function Scroll_To()
{
    window.scrollTo(0, 450);
}
```

I have verified that the function is being called. How do I make scrollTo work in IE6 and Opera?

A: The following code works in IE/Opera/Netscape/Mozilla with NO DOCTYPE set:

```
<html>
<head><script>
function Scroll_To(`)
{
    window.onload = Scroll_To;
}
</script></head>
<body onload='Scroll_To();'>
<pre>
```

```
Hello...

...World!</pre>
</body></html>
```

Then add:

```
<!DOCTYPE HTML PUBLIC "-//W3C//DTD HTML 4.01
Transitional//EN"
                "http://www.w3.org/TR/html4/loose.dtd">
```

to the top of the HTML, and it will still work.

Question 43: Refer to a TR Tag

How can I refer to an HTML row in JavaScript? If I add an id to it like <tr id="Age"></tr>, can I refer to it through document.forms[0].Age ?

A: Try the following:

```
var rowObj = document.getElementById("Age");
```

Question 44: Validate Multiple Email Addresses

I use the following code to validate an email address:

```
email=document.addUser.eMail.value;
var expression=/^([a-zA-Z0-9\-\._]+)@(([a-zA-Z0-9\-_]+\.)+)([a-z]{2,3})$/;
if(!(expression.test(email)) )
{
    alert("Please enter a valid email address (50
chars max)");
    document.addUser.eMail.select();
    document.addUser.eMail.focus();
    return false;
}
```

It works very nicely, but I want to alter it to validate several addresses. These addresses will come in the form of a commer delimites string from an <input type="text"> form element.

How do I rewrite the code to make it validate multiple email addresses?

A: You can try the following:

```
var expression=/^(([a-zA-Z0-9\-\._]+)@(([a-zA-Z0-9\-_]+\.)+)([a-z]{2,3})(,(?!$))?)+$/;
```

To allow for either a comma or semi-colon separator, replace "," with "[,;]".

To allow one space between the separator and the next address (a nice feature, but is not really essential), but not any space before the separator, replace "[,;]" with "[,;]\W?". (Further relaxation which might not be desirable would be for instance "\W?[,;]\W?" or much more "\W*[,;]\W*" along the same reasoning.)

```
var expression=/^(([a-zA-Z0-9\-\._]+)@(([a-zA-Z0-9\-_]+\.)+)([a-z]{2,3})([,;]\W?(?!$))?)+$/;
```

Question 45: Open Link in Parent Window

I have a page that is opened with a makeNewWindow() function from the original page. On this page, there are a few links that point to other pages. I want to be able to close the new window and open the link in the original window when a link is clicked.

How is it possible to open up a link in a parent window?

A: Your JavaScript solution would be:

```
<a href="mylink.html"
onclick="opener.location=this.href; window.close();
return false;">Click Me</a>
```

Question 46: Select the "i"th Value in a List Box

I have a list box which is generated from a SQL query. How do I select a specific value using an offset, i.e., select the 1st value?

A: Try this:

```
document.forms["formName"].elements["selectName"].sel
ectedIndex = offsetValue;
```

Question 47: Simple Checkbox

When one checkbox is selected, I want to make sure another one is unchecked. How do I write the code?

A: A radio button serves the purpose but you can also do the following:

```
<input name="cb1" type="checkbox" onclick="if
(this.checked) this.form.cb2.checked = false;" />
<input name="cb2" type="checkbox" onclick="if
(this.checked) this.form.cb1.checked = false;" />
```

Question 48: Get a Pop-up to Print

I have a function that scripts out HTML and JavaScript for two buttons: Close and Print. My close button works fine. When I try to use my print button, however, nothing happens.

The print button is supposed to generate a pop-up window to display information specifically for printing. The page the pop-up is launched from calls the external JavaScript function that takes the information to display as text and scripts out the entire HTML when it creates the page. Strangely enough, if I refresh the pop-up after pressing the print button, then my print dialog will open, almost as if the page is playing catch-up.

The function that creates my new page is as follows:

```
function printerfriendly(displayhtml)
{
  generator=window.open('/print.html','name','height=
400,width=500,menubar=yes,titlebar=yes,scrollbars=1,r
esizable=yes');

  start_erase = displayhtml.lastIndexOf('<P style',
displayhtml.indexOf('pfgraphic'));

  end_erase = displayhtml.indexOf('</P>',
displayhtml.indexOf('pflink'))+4;

  mystring =
```

```
displayhtml.replace(displayhtml.substring(start_erase
, end_erase),'') + '<center><input type="button"
value="Close"
onclick="javascript:window.close()"></input><input
type="Button" value="Print"
onclick="javascript:window.print()"></input></center>
';


  generator.document.write('<html>');
  generator.document.write('<head>');
  generator.document.write('</head>');
  generator.document.write('<body>');
  generator.document.write(mystring);
  generator.document.write('</body>');
  generator.document.write('</html>');
}
```

This function is called from another page when the user clicks on the appropriate link. It constructs then opens the pop-up page. Most of this code takes in the HTML I want for the pop-up and cuts the other out. The text in bold is the definition of the Print button on the pop-up.

What is wrong with the code?

A: Try a generator.document.open() immediately before your first call to the write() function and a generator.document.close() immediately after your last call to the write() function.

Question 49: Automate Word in JavaScript

I want to open a document in Word, print it, and then close Word. I have this working, but I want to make sure that the document is opened read-only. In VB, I would:

```
dim oWord
set oWord = createobject("word.application")
oword.documents.open "c:\mydocs\testdoc.doc",,true
```

The last parameter to the documents.open specifies that the doc be opened as read-only. In JavaScript, I have:

```
var oWord = new ActiveXObject("Word.Application");
oWord.Visible=true;
oWord.Documents.Open("c:\\mydocs\\testdoc.doc");
oWord.PrintOut(true);
oWord.Quit();
```

The JavaScript doesn't like having any additional parameters to the oWord.Documents.Open method.

How do I correct the code?

A: Try this:

```
oWord.Documents.Open("c:\\mydocs\\testdoc.doc",
false, true);
```

Question 50: Onclick-Session Variable

I have an ASP page that has a DELETE button on it. I also have a confirm message box showing via the onclick using JavaScript.

```
onclick="javascript: if session("xyz")
confirm("message 1") else confirm("message 2")
[\code]
```

Is it possible to have the onclick check a session variable, and then based on that variable, use one of two confirm messages?

A: Session variables are stored server side, so you will have to reference them as though they are server side. Using ASP:

```
onclick="javascript: if (<%=session("xyz")%>)
confirm("message 1") else confirm("message 2")
```

Question 51: Fill in a Form With a Hyperlink

I have one box called StartDate and one called EndDate. I also have a hyperlink which says 'Last 7 days'. I can use ASP to get a value for today's date and the date 7 days ago and embed those values in the hyperlink. Is it possible to fill in two form fields with a hyperlink and without reloading the page? How do I pass them to the form?

A: Yes, you can. Here is an example using a button and using href link:

```
<form name="myForm" action="">
<input name="start" type="text">
<input name="end" type="text">
<!-- using a button -->
<input type="button"
onclick="setStartEndDates('13/5/2005','20/5/2005');"
value="Set dates">
<!-- using a href -->
<a
href="javascript:setStartEndDates('13/5/2005','20/5/2
```

```
005');;>Set dates</a>
</form>

<script type="text/javascript">
function setStartEndDates(_start, _end) {
  var f = document.forms['myForm'];
  if (_start != '') f.elements['start'].value =
_start;
  if (_end!= '') f.elements['end'].value = _end;
}
</script>
```

Question 52: Change Text in Span

With the following script:

```
<SPAN ID="SPAN"></SPAN>
<INPUT TYPE=BUTTON VALUE="Change text"
ONCLICK="Text()">
<SCRIPT LANGUAGE="JavaScript">
function Text()
{document.getElementById("SPAN") = "New text";}
</SCRIPT>
```

How can I change text in a span?

A: Use the following:

```
>{document.getElementById("SPAN") = "New text";}
{document.getElementById("SPAN").innerHTML = "New
text";}
```

Question 53: Parse XML

I need to extract values and put t ext into 3 variables, one for each tag. This is in IE so Microsoft XML can be used.

```
<test>
<country>brazil</country>
<town>rio</town>
<person>
<name>ronaldo</name>
<name>socrates</name>
<name>zico</name>
<name>pele</name>
</person>
</test>
```

How do I parse the above XML in JavaScript so I can get the text?

A: You did not explain where you get the file. Supposing it is already read as textstream into a variable and work from there, you can try the following:

```
var sxml="<test>\r\n" +
    "<country>brazil</country>\r\n" +
    "\t<town>rio</town>\r\n" +
    "\t<person>\r\n" +
    "\t\t<name>ronaldo</name>\r\n" +
    "\t\t<name>socrates</name>\r\n" +
    "\t\t<name>zico</name>\r\n" +
    "\t\t<name>pele</name>\r\n" +
    "\t</person>\r\n" +
    "</test>";
var oparser=new ActiveXObject("Msxml2.DOMDocument");
oparser.loadXML (sxml);
var
scountry=oparser.selectSingleNode("/test/country").te
xt;
var
stown=oparser.selectSingleNode("/test/town").text;
var operson=oparser.selectSingleNode("/test/person");
var aoname=operson.childNodes
//this shows you what you get and how to retrieve
names
alert(socuntry + "\n" + stown + "\n" + aoname.length
```

```
+ "\n" + aoname[0].text + "\n"+aoname[1].text +
"\n"+aoname[2].text + "\n" + aoname[3].text);
```

Question 54: JS Not Showing 0 (Zero) Values in Text Box

I have recently created the following JS which works perfectly except it is not showing the 0 (zeros) values in the targeted text box.

```
if (prempack == 4)
    {
        premsum = 20.00;
    }
    thisform.premoutput.value = premsum;
and text box

<input type="text" name="premoutput" size="4"
readonly="true"/>
```

For example, a 0.00 value does not show anything and 13.50 shows as 13.5 . How do I show the zero values in the text box?

A: Use the toFixed method:
(passing the number of decimals as the argument)

```
<script type="text/javascript">
var a = 1.10;
alert("normal: " + a + "\ntoFixed: " + a.toFixed(2));
</script>
```

Question 55: Change Web Content Daily

I do not want to pay my Webmaster to manually change web content for me daily. Is there a service that would do this (such as set a different jpeg everyday)? Or is this possible with JavaScript if I give my Webmaster a database?

A: If you have server side scripting available, you can use that to handle changing the graphic automatically. JavaScript can do that too, but it won't work for people who have it disabled in their browsers.

Question 56: Print Value of Entries Using for Loop

The following code will print 3 literals with each fieldname only, but not the values.

```
<script>
function myT()
{
for(var i=1;i<4;i++)
{
    alert("document.tes.firstname"+[i]+".value");
    //The below alert wont alert anything
    //alert(document.tes.firstname[i].value);
}

}

</script>
<form name="tes" method="post"
action="actionPage.cfm" onsubmit="return myT();">
<input type="Text" name="firstname1">
<input type="Text" name="firstname2">
<input type="Text" name="firstname3">
<input type="Submit" value="submit">
</form>
```

The script Pops up 3 alerts with literal field names:
document.tes.firstname1.value
document.tes.firstname2.value

```
document.tes.firstname3.value
```

I want it to pop up 3 alerts with each value entered. Currently it goes through the "for" loop and prints the literal values.

How do I get the values entered to print out in my alert using a for loop?

A: The forms and elements collections will solve your problems.

```
function myT() {
    for(var i = 1; i < 4; i++) {
        alert(document.forms["tes"].elements["firstname
" + i].value);
    }
}
```

Or to get all the values at once, store them into a variable and then output at the end instead of having a bunch of pop-ups.

```
function myT() {
   var outstr='';
   for(var i = 1; i < 4; i++) {
     outstr = outstr +
document.forms["tes"].elements["firstname" + i].value
+ '\r\n';
   }
   alert(outstr);
}
```

Question 57: Append to a List

I'm trying to create a list for which every time the code is executed, it appends the new values to the end of the list. I have tried the following but it always returns null.

```
if(listXY == null)
{
  alert("list eq null");
  var listXY=clickedX+","+clickedY;
}
else
{
  alert("list eq summit");
  listXY=","+listXY+","+clickedX+","+clickedY;
}
```

How do I resolve this issue?

A: You need to declare your variable listXY as a global variable. Don't declare it local to the function.

```
var listXY = null; // outside the function

function somefunc() {

if(listXY == null)
{
  alert("list eq null");
  ~~var~~ listXY=clickedX+","+clickedY;
}
else
{
  alert("list eq summit");
  listXY=","+listXY+","+clickedX+","+clickedY;
}


}
```

Question 58: Refresh Parent Window When Pop-up is Closed

With the following code, I would like to close the pop-up window when the close button is clicked, and then refresh the parent window so all the updated details show.

```
<script
language="JavaScript">window.close();</script>

<script
language="JavaScript">window.opener.location.reload()
;</script>
```

However, when the site is posted live, the script closes the top window and seems to reload the same window. How should I write the code to refresh the parent window when the pop-up window is closed?

A: You can try to do something like this:

```
<a href="#" onclick="opener.location.reload(true);
window.close(); return false;">Close Me</a>
```

Question 59: Validate Currency Values

Some of my fields in the form are currency fields and I need to add some validations around it to make it "dummy proof".

```
<tr>
<td>Annual Revenue, if known ($):</td>
<td><input type=text style="width: 285px;"
class="textbox" name="business_rev" size=20
maxlength="12" value=""
onChange="document.frm.business_rev.value=commaSplit(
document.frm.business_rev.value);">
</td>
</tr>
```

For example, I want this field to accept a maximum of 12 numbers and the values are formatted with a script to make the value look like 000,000,000,000. I accomplished this with the following code:

```
<SCRIPT LANGUAGE="JavaScript">

<!-- Begin
function commaSplit(srcNumber) {
var txtNumber = '' + srcNumber;
if (isNaN(txtNumber) || txtNumber == "") {
alert("That does not appear to be a valid
number.  Please try again.");
fieldName.select();
fieldName.focus();

}
else {
var rxSplit = new RegExp('([0-9])([0-9][0-9][0-
9][,.])');
var arrNumber = txtNumber.split('.');
arrNumber[0] += '.';
do {
arrNumber[0] = arrNumber[0].replace(rxSplit,
'$1,$2');
} while (rxSplit.test(arrNumber[0]));
if (arrNumber.length > 1) {
return arrNumber.join('');
}
else {
return arrNumber[0].split('.')[0];
```

```
      }
    }
}
//  End -->
</script>
```

However, if, for instance, I enter 1111111111.25, the form should still accept that as 12 values and not 13.

How can I make it accept "periods" without counting it as part of the 12 values?

A: You will need to dynamically set the maxlength attribute based upon whether you detect a '.' in the value or not. You'll probably need to do this in the onKeyDown event with something like this:

```
onkeydown="checkMaxLength(this);
```

with this script:

```
function checkMaxLength(formEl) {
    if (formEl.value.indexOf('.') != -1) {
       formEl.maxLength = '12';
    } else {
       formEl.maxLength = '13';
    }
}
```

Question 60: Retrieve Value From onClick of a Table Row

I am currently designing a JSP page that will retrieve a list of customers and display them in a data-grid type table.

The specs call for tabs to be placed at the top of the table, which will allow the user to view specific info about a customer they have selected from the table (by onClick of the table row).

What I would like to do is to somehow take the unique database ID # of each customer and pass it to a link for the "Customer Details" tab. Basically, you click a record row and the tab is given a link, something like view_customer.jsp?id=346.

Here's what I've started with:

```
for( int x = 0; x < patientList.length; x++ ) {
    out.write("<tr>");
    out.write("    <td
class=\"gridColumn\">"+patientList[x].getPTID()+"<inp
ut type=\"hidden\" name=\"ptNum\" id=\"ptNum\"
value=\""+patientList[x].getPTNO()+"\"></td>");
    out.write("    <td
class=\"gridColumn\">"+patientList[x].getPTLNAME()+"<
/td>");
    out.write("    <td
class=\"gridColumn\">"+patientList[x].getPTFNAME()+"<
/td>");
    out.write("    <td
class=\"gridColumn\">"+patientList[x].getPTADD1()+"</
td>");
    out.write("    <td
class=\"gridColumn\">"+patientList[x].getPTCITY()+"</
td>");
    out.write("    <td
class=\"gridColumn\">"+patientList[x].getPTSTATE()+"<
/td>");
    out.write("    <td
class=\"gridColumn\">"+patientList[x].getPTZIP()+"</t
d>");
    out.write("</tr>");
  }
```

How can I improve this code?

A: If your tab has a link in it, with an ID of, for example, "myTab":

```
<a href="javascript:alert('You need to select a row
first!');" id="myTab">Click here to dance the
Agadoo</a>
```

Then you could skip the input field, and just set the URL directly:

```
<td onlick="document.getElementById('myTab').href =
'view_customer.jsp?id=' + patientList[x].getPTID();"
...>
```

Note the default alert "if no row" is selected.

Question 61: HTML Editor

What I am trying to achieve is to give flexibility to the user (i.e., to be able to select different fonts, size, colors, create hyperlinks, etc.).

Does anybody know of a free HTML editor I can use (in place of <TEXTAREA>)?

A: Two options would be FCKEdit and TinyMCE.

Question 62: Cookies and JavaScript Support

I need to paste a page on mywebsite for people to test if they have JS and cookies enabled. Kind of like "click here to see if you have JS and cookies enabled".

How do I write the code for this kind of test?

A: For the JS, that's dead easy:

```
<a href="javascript:alert('You have JavaScript
enabled');">Click this link, and if you see no
message, you have JavaScript disabled</a>
```

For the cookies, you'll need to first make sure they have JavaScript enabled, and then write a cookie, and read it back. If it does not read back, you know they're disabled.

Question 63: onChange Event Handler in IE 6.x

I wrote a simple script that will disable a group of <select> form elements based on the value on another <select>. It works fine in Opera and FF. In IE 6.x, however, I can make the function fire once, but if I change the select option again, nothing happens.

Here's the function:

```
function disableDelay(){
            if
(document.connectionType.periodicUpdates.value=="No")
{
                document.connectionType.updateDelay.d
isabled=true;
            } else
document.connectionType.updateDelay.disabled=false;

Here's where I call the function:
```

```
<select name="periodicUpdates"
onChange=disableDelay() >
            <option
<%=(synchronizationSettingBoolean) ? "selected" :
""%> >Yes</option>
            <option
<%=(synchronizationSettingBoolean) ? "" :
"selected"%> >No</option>
        </select>
```

How can I make this work in IE?

A: Provide VALUE attributes for your options.

```
<option <%=(synchronizationSettingBoolean) ?
"selected" : ""%> value='Yes'>Yes</option>
<option <%=(synchronizationSettingBoolean) ? "" :
"selected"%> value='No'>No</option>
```

Question 64: Get Value from Select Field

The following code returns undefined.

```
<html>
<head>
<title>New Page 10</title>
 <script Language="JavaScript"><!--
function checkData()
    {
        var myTest  = me.D1.selectedIndex.value;
    alert(myTest);
    }
</script>
</head>

<body>
<form method="POST" name="me">
    <select size="1"
name="D1"  onChange="checkData()">
    <option value="99">Default</option>
    <option value="1">1</option>
```

```
<option value="2">2</option>
<option value="3">3</option>
<option value="4">4</option>
</select><input type="submit" value="Submit"
name="B1"><input type="reset" value="Reset"
name="B2"></p>
</form>
</body>
</html>
```

How do I get the value for the selected option?

A: "selectedIndex", when used correctly, returns the index (number) of the space in the options collection in which the selected option resides. Here's what you may want to use:

```
me.D1.options[me.D1.selectedIndex].value
```

or

```
me.D1.options[me.D1.options.selectedIndex].value
```

Question 65: Highlight Keywords onClick Hyperlink

I work for a school and I'm trying to write some learning materials, which include differentiation for Special Needs students. The idea is that there will be a task displayed in a box on the screen (all in HTML) and a link at the bottom saying 'Highlight keywords'. When a student clicks the link, it will highlight the important words in the task to help special needs students understand the important parts of the task.

Do you know how I can do this? I presume JavaScript is the easiest way.

A: You can do it a number of ways.

The first that comes to mind is to pull the innerHTML value of the section you want the highlighting done in, parsing through the text, looking for the keywords and then adding tags to those words to alter their style and spitting then writing the innerHTML value back out updated.

Another approach would be to set a style for those keywords to set the highlighting. Normally, you could have one default style set for them and with the click of a button on the screen just change the style or class that applies to those elements.

Here is a very simple page that shows a way to do this. When the "toggle" link is clicked, it loops through the whole page looking for <span> tags with a class of "spec" (you c an change these to whatever you use). When it finds a span with a matching class, it checks to see if the contents are color "red"... and if so, it sets them to black/normal (otherwise it sets them to red/bold):

```
<html>
<head>
<script type="text/javascript">
function toggle() {
  var _collection =
document.getElementsByTagName('span');
  for (var loop = 0, max = _collection.length; loop <
max; loop++) {
    if (_collection[loop].className == "spec") {
      if (_collection[loop].style.color == "red") {
        _collection[loop].style.color = "black";
        _collection[loop].style.fontWeight =
"normal";
      } else {
        _collection[loop].style.color = "red";
        _collection[loop].style.fontWeight = "bold";
      }
    }
  }
}
</script>
</head>
<body>
<div class="hint">Turn off the <span
class="spec">computer off</span> by first <span
class="spec">turning off the power switch</span> and
then <span class="spec">pulling out the power
cord</span></div>
<a href="javascript:toggle();">Toggle</a>
</body>
</html>
```

Question 66: Variable in Form Change

```
<script language="JavaScript" type="text/javascript">
<!--
function getFName(browse, attach)
{
var path;
var pos;
var filename;
var jar;
path = browse;
pos=path.lastIndexOf("\\");
filename = path.substring(pos+1);
alert(filename)

jar="attach1"
document.frmSend.+jar+.value=filename;

}

//-->
</script>
```

How do I modify the above code so that I can pass a form element that will be called through ASP?

A: Try this:

```
document.forms['frmSend'].elements[jar].value=filenam
e;
```

Question 67: One Click, Two URLs

I have a download page where people can choose from several brochures (PDFs). When they click on the brochure, I want it to pop open a new window with the PDF, and the background brochure page to switch to a thank you page.

Here's what I tried:

```
<a target="_blank" href="brochures/#strFilename#"
onClick="parent.frames[0].location.href='brochuresTha
nkYou.cfm';">#strTitle#</a>
```

(Brochure listings are being fed from a database via coldfusion, that's why the #'s.)

I have no iframes or frameset at all. All I have is the background page going to a thank you page, and the PDF popping up. People without JavaScript can just get the PDF. Basically, the thank you page will be tracking my Google PPC campaign.

How do I rewrite the above code to make it work?

A: Try this:

```
<a href="brochures/#strFilename#"
onclick="window.open(this.href, '', ''); this.href =
'brochuresThankYou.cfm'; this.target = '';"
target="_blank">#strTitle#</a>
```

Question 68: Calling a Given Function

I am trying to get an iframe to load different local pages at a given interval with the following code:

```
<script language="javascript">
    function rotate() {
        var urls= new Array (2);
        urls[0]="page0.html";
        urls[1]="page1.html";
        urls[2]="page2.html";

        document.getElementById('displayFrame').src =
URLS[0];
    }
</script>
```

Is there a timer sort of function that I can use to make this iframe loop through this array and display the html pages one by one (looping back to the first element after reaching the end)?

A: Yes, it's called "setTimeout(...)". It takes two parameters. The first is a String that tells the function what to do. The second is a number that tells it how long to wait (in milliseconds) to do it.

For example:

```
function cycleThrough()
{
  for(var i=0; i<urls.length; i++)
  {
   setTimeout("document.getElementById('displayFrame')
.src = urls["+i+"];", 1000*i);
  }
}
```

i	first param	second param
0	urls[0]	0
1	urls[1]	1000
2	urls[2]	2000

Now, if you want the process to be forever continuous:

```
var iteration = 0;
function cycleThrough()
{
  document.getElementById('displayFrame').src =
urls[iteration];
  iteration++;
  if(iteration == urls.length)
   iteration = 0;
  setTimeout("cycleThrough();", 1000);
}
```

This calls itself, every second (1000 milliseconds), and does the src-setting with each successive index of the array.

Question 69: JavaScript: Reading From a File/Generating GUID

I need to generate a unique GUID {xxxx-xxxx-xxxx-xxxx-xxxx-xxxx-xxxx} from client-side. Since I am not able to figure out how to do this on JAVASCRIPT Client-side, I figured that maybe I can (from client-side) open a file (say: http://www.aDifferentDomain.com/GUIDGenerator.asp) and read the GUID off it (which is generated dynamically).

My script will be running from a different domain from the GUIDGenerator.asp. The GUIDGenerator.asp will output just a line of GUID.

I am also trying to make it generic, i.e., can be run on any browser and not just MS IE. How can this be done?

A: If you make your ASP page output the GUID in a JS string:

```
var myGUID = '{xxxx-xxxx-xxxx-xxxx-xxxx-xxxx-xxxx}';
```

then you can simply use the ASP page as a JS include file:

```
<script type="text/javascript"
src="guidGenerator.asp"></script>
```

and then use the variable "myGUID".

Question 70: RegExp Hex Color

```
var string="blah #000000 test #FF0000 blah #eeff00";
```

I know that "\d{6} " is six digits but it's not always digits only. Could you tell me the regular expression for matching hex color codes?

A: Try this:

```
\#[0-9A-F]{6}
```

Don't forget ignorecase, or #abcdef won't work.

Question 71: Function Working in FF but Not in IE

This code works in Firefox but not in IE:

```
function get_balance() {

var start_amt =
document.forms[0].start_amt_toward_debt.value;
var total_payment = 0;
var percent_owed = 0;
var payment_amt = 0;
var total_owed = 0.00;

for(i=0; i<15; i++) {
    myBalance = 'balance'+i;
        if(parseFloat(document.getElementById(myBalan
ce).value)) {
            total_owed =
parseFloat(document.getElementById(myBalance).value)
+ total_owed ;
        }
    }
    for(i=0; i<15; i++) {
        myBalance = 'balance'+i;
        myPayment = 'p_payment'+i;
        creditor_amt =
```

```
parseFloat(document.getElementById(myBalance).value);
        percent_owed = (creditor_amt / total_owed) ;
        payment_amt = (start_amt * percent_owed) ;

        if (payment_amt > 0) {
            document.forms[0].eval(myPayment).value =
round(payment_amt) ;
            total_payment += payment_amt ;
        } else {
            document.forms[0].eval(myPayment).value =
'' ;
        }
    }

    document.forms[0].total_balance.value =
round(total_owed) ;
}
```

NOTE: round() is a JavaScript function that works.

What is causing the problem?

A: Try this:

```
document.forms[0].elements[myPayment].value
```

Question 72: Dynamic Update of Text Input

I want to be able to update the value of one text box when another is changed. I have tried the following and keep getting errors.

```
function DollarAmount(quantity) {
    document.eraffle.Amount.value = ((quantity*5) -
(cint(quantity/5)*5));}
```

```
<td class="BodyText">
        <input name="NoTicket" type="text"
id="NoTicket" size="4" maxlength="4"
onchange="DollarAmount(NoTicket.value)"
value="1"></td>
<td><input type="text" name="Amount" value=""></td>
```

The td tags are actually inside a complete table, I just pasted the important bits here. How do I correct the errors?

A: You can choose from the following:

```
[1]
>document.eraffle.Amount.value = ((quantity*5) -
(cint(quantity/5)*5));}
document.eraffle.Amount.value = ((quantity*5) -
(parseInt(quantity/5,10)*5));}
or you more probably meant for this direct
corresponding with cint().
document.eraffle.Amount.value = ((quantity*5) -
(Math.floor(quantity/5)*5));}
```

```
[2]
>onchange="DollarAmount(NoTicket.value)"
onchange="DollarAmount(this.value)"
```

Question 73: Check Dynamic Checkboxes

Say you want to make sure the first checkbox in the form is checked before submitting the form. How do I check if the checkbox is checked if I don't necessarily know the name or ID of the checkbox, which was dynamically created?

A: Use the getElementsByTagName collection to grab all inputs and then check to make sure the type is checkbox. Here's an example:

```
<html>
<head>
<script type="text/javascript">

function createCheckbox() {
    document.getElementById("theDiv").innerHTML =
"<input type=\"checkbox\" />checkbox1<br /><input
type=\"checkbox\" />checkbox2";
}

function validateMe(frm) {
    chks = document.getElementsByTagName("input");
    var i = 0;
    for (i = 0; i < chks.length; i++) {
        //check to see if we found the FIRST checkbox
        if (chks[i].type == "checkbox") {
            //check to see if the first checkbox was
checked
            if (chks[i].checked) {
                alert("first checkbox on the form was
checked, submission proceeding");
                return true;
            }
            else {
                alert("the first checkbox on the form
must be checked when submitting");
                return false;
            }
        }
    }
    alert("no checkboxes found");
    return false;
}
```

```
</script>
</head>

<body onload="createCheckbox()">
   <form onsubmit="return validateMe(this)"
method="get" action="">
      <div id="theDiv"></div>
      <input type="submit" value="submit me" />
   </form>
</body>
</html>
```

Question 74: Pass a Variable

```
<script language="JavaScript">
temp= window.prompt ("Please Type Your Name");
</script>
<script>
function initialize()
{
 document.forms['form'].elements['email'].value = ("+
temp +");
}
</script>
```

I tried this but in the variable I get + temp + in the fields that I want the value of the variable temp. Is it possible to pass a variable from one JavaScript to another JavaScript in the same html page?

A: Try this instead:

```
document.forms['form'].elements['email'].value =
temp;
```

And make sure you're not trying to access the variable before it's being defined.

Question 75: Images

I have a number of buttons that change an image as the user passes the mouse over each button. The function works great on my local PC, but fails to show the images when I access my site on the server. I am not receiving an error message; the image just fails to display. What am I missing?

A: Some possibilities include:
- incorrect path to the image
- incorrect case (filenames on UNIX servers are case sensitive: the case used in the img src must match that used on the server)
- slow loading (in which case you'll want to preload the images).

Question 76: Get Length from getElementsFromTagName Array

I want to get the string length of a hyperlink from the getElementsByTagName array, but the alert keeps saying undefined. I tried to create an array in the code itself and I was able to get the length of the element. Here is the code:

```
<html>
<head>
<style type="text/css">
a{color:red;background:orange}
.goo:first-letter{font-size:16pt;color:darkblue}
</style>
<script language=javascript>
function tt(){
AA = document.getElementsByTagName('a');
CC = AA.length;
teen = new Array();
for(TT = 0;TT < AA.length;TT++)
{
teen[TT] = AA[TT]
}

alert(teen[0].length)
}
```

```
</script>

</head>
<body onLoad=tt()>
<div align=center>
<a href="http://www.linkone.com">emuasy</a><P>
<a href="http://www.ebay.com">ebay</a><P>
<a href="http://www.yahoo.com">yahoo</a>
</div>
<div class=goo>
this is just a test to see if something will change
or not </div>
</body>
</html>
```

What is the problem with the above code?

A: Try the following changes:

>alert(teen[o].length) should be: alert(teen.length)

teen[o] is the reference to the first anchor element itself.

For the string length of a hyperlink, maybe this is what you're looking for:

   alert(teen[o].innerHTML.length);

or

   alert(teen[o].href.length);

Question 77: Join Variable to Textbox Name

I want to join this variable varWID in the name of the texbox, but I'm not sure what to search for.

```
<script type="text/javascript">
function copydata(varWID)
{
document.FRMadds.wopenwidth.value =
document.FRMadds.wopenwidth + varWID +.value;
}
</script>
```

How do I rewrite my code?

A: Change the following:

```
>document.FRMadds.wopenwidth.value =
document.FRMadds.wopenwidth + varWID +.value;
```

to

```
document.FRMadds.wopenwidth.value =
document.FRMadds.elements["wopenwidth" +
varWID].value;
```

Question 78: Display Form

I have two different login systems: login A and login B. If possible, I want to have two radio buttons that will display a login form (username and password) but send the login information to different places based on the radio that is selected. So, for instance, if A is selected when the user entered their username and password it will send their information to /A/login.html or if b /B/login.html.

How do I write the code?

A: Use the form's onsubmit handler to switch the action tag of the form depending on what was checked:

```
<script type="text/javascript">
function blah(theForm) {
   var radios = theForm.elements["rad"];
   if (radios[0].checked) {
      theForm.action = "./a/login.html";
   }
   else {
      theForm.action = "./b/login.html";
   }
   return true;
}
</script>
<body>
<form method="post" id="frm" onsubmit="return
blah(this)" action="">
   <input type="radio" value="a" name="rad" />a<br />
   <input type="radio" value="b" name="rad" />a<br />
   <input type="text" id="txt"><br />
   <input type="submit" value="submit me">
</form>
</body>
```

Question 79: Set SELECT selectedIndex Same Over There

I have 2 dropdowns and I want to set the selectedIndex of the second select to be the same as the first.

```
onChange="setDDLVals(this,frmConfig.selThis2);"
```

```
function setDDLVals(ddl1,that)
{
    that.options[that.selectedIndex] =
ddl1.options[ddl1.selectedIndex];
}
```

However, I get the following error message:

Property doesn't support JS code

How do I correct this?

A: Try:

```
that.selectedIndex = ddl1.selectedIndex;
```

Question 80: JavaScript in IE vs Firefox

Using event listeners, I have attached a blur event to a set of text fields. So, when I move out of any of these text boxes, the blur event fires. This calls a function called Checkvalues(), which checks the value of the current control. If the controls data is incorrect, I want to reset the focus to this control.

I am doing this with the following code:

```
var errorMessage = CheckTaskValue(control);

                                        if(errorM
essage!=null)
                                {
                        alert(errorMessage);
                        control.focus();

                }
```

In IE, this works fine, however, in Firefox, it doesn't refocus.

What am I doing wrong?

A: Put the focus call in a setTimeout call with a really small delay (say, 50 msecs).

Question 81: Href Tags

Is there any way that I can collate all a href links within the body of an html page and store them in some sort of list?

A: This will work:

```
<html>
<head>
    <script type="text/javascript">
    <!--
        onload = collateLinks;

        function collateLinks() {
            var outputStr = '';
            var allLinks =
document.getElementsByTagName('a');
            for (var loop=0; loop<allLinks.length;
loop++) {
                outputStr += 'Link URL: ' +
allLinks[loop].href + '\nLink Content: ' +
allLinks[loop].innerHTML + '\n\n';
            }
            alert(outputStr);
        }

    //-->
    </script>
</head>

<body>
    <a href="somelink.html">link text</a>
    <a href="somelink2.html">more link text</a>
</body>
</html>
```

Question 82: Cannot Load XML File

I want to dynamically load an XML file using a generic xslt with the following code:

```javascript
<script language="javascript">

    var xmlfile = "file.xml";
    var param = null;

    if (location.search.length > 0)
    {
        param =
location.search.substring(1).split("?");
    }

    if (param == xmlfile)
    {
        alert("identical");
    }

        var xml = new
ActiveXObject("Microsoft.XMLDOM");
        xml.async = false;
        var xsl = new
ActiveXObject("Microsoft.XMLDOM");
        xsl.async = false;


    // Load XML
    //xml.load(xmlfile);
    xml.load(param);

    // Load the XSL
    xsl.load("UCMReport.xsl");

    // Transform
    document.write(xml.transformNode(xsl));
</script>
```

If I hardcode the XML filename, it works fine. However, when I get this filename from my URL as a parameter www.zzz.com\load.html?file.xml, it does not load the file.

If I comment out xml.load(param); and use xmlfile for the load function, it works.

Worst of all, each time I run the script, I get my pop-up saying that those 2 variables have identical values.

How do I make it work?

A: When you use split(), you get an array of parts. Since you apparently want the base URL and not any excess stuff after the "?", try this:

```
if (location.search.length > 0)
{
     param =
location.search.substring(1).split("?")[0];
}
```

Question 83: Dynamic Events on Dynamic Controls

I am trying to do the following (actions and events are actually sent in a function):

```
events = 'onClick,onSubmit'
actions = 'alert("submitting"),subform()'
events = events.split(",")
actions = actions.split(",")
for(i=0;i<events.length;i++){
frmEle[events[i]]=function() {eval(actions[i])}
```

If I do frmEle.onClick=function() {eval(actions[i])}, it works, but I can't seem to add the event dynamically.

How can I add the event dynamically?

A: Try:

```
eval('frmEle.' + events[i] + ' = function() { ' +
actions[i] + '}');
```

Question 84: Dropdown Boxes - mail to

I'd like to place a dropdown box on a website with several 'mail me' names such as: sales, webmaster, complaints, etc.

```
<html>
<head>
<meta http-equiv="Content-Type" content="text/html;
charset=windows-1252">
<title>New Page 1</title>
</head>
<body>
<!-- Add this to the <head> section -->
<script language="JavaScript" type="text/javascript">
function GotoURL() {
location.href=document.go.picker[document.go.picker.s
electedIndex].value;}</script>
<!-- Add this to the <body> section -->
<!-- Obviously, you should edit the code to show your
own URLs, and you can change the style attributes to
suit your colour scheme -->
<form name="go" id="go">
<select name="picker" id="picker" style="font-family:
Arial, Helvetica, sans-serif;">
<option value="index3.htm" style="background-color:
#e0e0e0;" selected>Home Page</option>
<option value="contents.htm">Contents</option>
<option value="feedback.htm" style="background-color:
#e0e0e0;">Webmaster</option>
<option value="tools.htm">Tools I use</option>
</select>
<input type="button" value="Go"
style="color:#FFFFFF;background:#CC9900" title="Click
to Go" onClick="GotoURL()">
</form>
</body>
</html>
```

How can I add something similar to:

```
<a
href="mailto:rupert.wilson@gmail.com">rupert.wilson@g
mail.com</a>
```

to each value ?

A: Try the following:

```
<html>
<head>
<meta http-equiv="Content-Type" content="text/html;
charset=windows-1252">
<title>New Page 1</title>
</head>
<body>
<!-- Add this to the <head> section -->
<script language="JavaScript" type="text/javascript">
function GotoURL() {
location.href="mailto:" +
document.getElementsByName("picker")[0].value;


}
</script>
<!-- Add this to the <body> section -->
<!-- Obviously, you should edit the code to show your
own URLs, and you can change the style attributes to
suit your colour scheme -->
<form name="go" id="go">
<select name="picker" id="picker" style="font-family:
Arial, Helvetica, sans-serif;">
<option value="hi@hi.com" style="background-color:
#e0e0e0;" selected>Home Page</option>
<option value="hello@hello.com">Contents</option>
<option value="goodbye@goodbye.com"
style="background-color: #e0e0e0;">Webmaster</option>
<option value="lol@lol.com">Tools I use</option>
</select>
<input type="button" value="Go"
style="color:#FFFFFF;background:#CC9900" title="Click
to Go" onClick="GotoURL()">
</form>
</body>
</html>
```

Question 85: Refresh HTML Page

I have a HTML/ASP page that has a text area that is populated from a pop-up window. When the user selects a date in the pop-up calendar, the date if filled into my current page. What I need for the current page to do is refresh when the date is changed. I have an onchange event in the field and it works if I type in a date, but not when it is auto filled from the pop-up.

Here is my code from the pop-up:

```
<a href="javascript:;"
onclick="opener.document.getElementById('<%=varFieldN
ame%>').value='<%=FormatDateTime(ThisDate)%>';
window.close();"
title="<%=FormatDateTime(ThisDate,1)%>"
class="CalDate"><%=DateNumber%></a>
```

Here is my text field:

```
<input
type="text"  name="SelectedDate"  onchange="document.
search.submit()" id="SelectedDate" maxlength="13"
size="12" value="<% =SelectedDate%>">
```

How do I get the page to refresh?

A: Before this:

```
window.close();
```

add this:

```
opener.document.search.submit();
```

Question 86: window.open Page in iframe

On a page that is already open in an iframe called "Mainframe", I have a button that has a JavaScript function attached to it:

```
onclick="var w = window.open('../Partitions/' +
this.form.txtlink.value, 'txtlink', 'Mainframe','')
```

It is set to open a page, of which the URL is generated out of ../partitions/+ the value of a textbox called txtlink.

How do I open a new page in the same frame?

A: This may be what you are looking for:

```
onclick="document.location='../Partitions/' +
this.form.txtlink.value;"
```

Question 87: Get Value of XML Node

I am trying to see whether the adding of a row to the db was a success or not using AJAX, so the server passes back an XML document:

```
<?xml version="1.0" encoding="UTF-8"?>
<root type='error'>
<message>success</message>
</root>
```

Is there a way to see what the value of <message> is?

A: If you're actually getting an XML DOM object back from the server, a la XMLHttpRequest.responseXML, then you should just be able to use DOM methods:

```
var msg =
```

```
oXml.getElementsByTagName("message")[0].firstChild.no
deValue;
```

Question 88: Image Swapper

I have two images. One is loaded as a default when the page is loaded. I want another image displayed when the user clicks on the image, and the clicked picture gets hidden. If the user clicks again, the old picture is displayed and the clicked one is hidden and so on. Do you have any suggestions to make this happen?

A: There are many ways of doing this, and none of them really has any benefit over the others so I'll give just one example. Put this in your script section:

```
var imagesToShow = ['myImage1.jpg', 'myImage2.jpg'];
var imageNumber = 0;
```

Obviously, put the filenames (or paths and filenames) of the two images in the imagesToShow array. Then, put an onclick attribute in your image element:

```
<img src="myImage1.jpg" onclick="this.src =
imagesToShow[imageNumber = Number(!imageNumber)];" />
```

Note: You've made no mention of requirements for differing widths, heights, alt or title tags, etc. I assumed that if you had wanted those features, you would have asked for them.

Question 89: Select Element

```
<script>
function setForm() {
    var _select = document.getElementById("x_opt");

    alert(_select.value);
        alert(_select.optionText); // I know this is
not correct
}
</script>

<select id="x_opt" name="x_opt"
onchange="setForm();">
    <option value="0">Option 0</option>
    <option value="1">Option 1</option>
    <option value="2">Option 2</option>
</select>
```

If option 0 was selected I would like to be alerted the value of 0 and the text of Option 0. How do you retrieve the text from a select element in the option portion?

A: The following is untested, but should be:

```
alert(_select.text);
```

or

```
alert(_select.options[_select.selectedIndex].text);
```

Question 90: Replace

I have text being entered into a text area. When it is submitted, I replace line returns with <br> to display correctly in the browser window. When someone wants to edit the text, I want to replace the <br> that were entered with a carriage return in the textarea to edit. How would I replace the
's with a carriage return in the textarea?

A: This should show the idea:

```
alert("tektips<br>rule".replace('<br>','\n\r'));
```

Question 91: Disable Button

I have a dropdown menu with items which can be multi-selected. There are two buttons on the page: button1 and button2. How can I disable button1 if I select more than 1 item in the dropdown menu?

A: Try this:

```
function doit(osel) {
    //this being the onchange handler of select
element
    //called with onchange="doit(this)"
    //form name: frmtest; input button name: btntest;

    var bselected=false
    for (var i=0;i<osel.length;i++) {
        if (osel.options[i].selected) {
            if (bselected) {
                document.frmtest.btntest.disabled=tru
e;
                return;
            } else {
                bselected=true;
            }
        }
    }
```

```
document.frmtest.btntest.disabled=false;
}
```

Question 92: Create an 'onMouseOver'

I want to create an image that when the mouseOver takes place, an alert comes up, but only once. How can I do that?

A: Have this in the script:

```
var didIt=false;
```

and send the mouseOver to this function:

```
function doMouseOvr(
if (!didIt){
alert('hehehehehe');
didIt=true;
}
}
```

with this, if, by some miracle, you want to do it again,

```
didIt=false;
doMouseOvr():
```

Question 93: Make Banner Frame Disappear

I have made a site with a banner at the top displaying a few links and the name of the site, e.g., http://www.ask.com.

What I want is that when you ask a question and click one of the answer links it leaves, the banner frame for navigation back to the site, (or to the question you asked), but allows you to close frame leaving the current page.

Is there any way to put a link (or button) on the banner so that when the user clicks it, the banner disappears leaving only the current page?

A: If the bottom frame tag has a name of "botframe" like this:

```
<frame name="botframe" ....>
```

Then in the top frame document you could do this:

```
function whatever_onclick() {

  window.top.location =
    window.top.frames("botframe").document.location;
}
```

Question 94: Textbox Should Go With Checkbox Value

I have a problem with assigning a value of Quantity in a textarea. When a user clicks a checkbox, the value of the checkbox and quantity should appear together in the textarea.

```
<script language="JavaScript">
<!--
function setField(theForm)
{
  theForm.quantity.value = 1;
    theForm.order.value = "";
    var val = "";
    for (var i=0; i<theForm.equipment.length; i++) ||
(var i=0; i<theForm.quantity.length; i++)
  {
        if
((theForm.equipment.name.indexOf('equipment') > -1))
  || ((theForm.quantity.name.indexOf('quantity') > -1))
  {
        if (theForm.equipment.checked) ||
theForm.quantity['quantity' + i].value
    {
          theForm.order.value +=
theForm.equipment.value + " - " +
theForm.quantity.value + "\n";
          }
        }
      }
  }
```

124

```
file://-->
</script>

<form name="order">
<input type="checkbox" name="equipment"
value="Printer" onClick="setField(this.form)">
<input type="text" name="quantity" value="1" size=2
onChange="setField(this.form)">
<br>
<input type="checkbox" name="equipment" value="Mouse"
onClick="setField(this.form)">
<input type="text" name="quantity" value="1" size=2
onChange="setField(this.form)">
<br>
<input type="checkbox" name="equipment"
value="Keyboard" onClick="setField(this.form)">
<input type="text" name="quantity" value="1" size=2
onChange="setField(this.form)">
<br>
<textarea onChange="setField(this.form)" name=order
value="?" rows=5></textarea>
<br>
</form>
```

However, this code doesn't function properly because I get the message that the value is undefined.

How can I correct this problem?

A: You can only give a group of radio buttons the same name. Your problem is that you are trying to access the values of three different textboxes that have the same name. Try this code:

```
<script language="JavaScript">
<!--
var iNumBoxes = 3;
function setField(theForm) {
    theForm.order.value = "";
    var val = "";
    for(var i = 0; i < iNumBoxes; i++) {
        if (theForm['equipment' + i].checked &&
theForm['quantity' + i].value > 0) {
            theForm.order.value += theForm['equipment' +
i].value + " - " + theForm['quantity' + i].value +
"\n";
        }
```

```
    }
}
file://-->
</script>

<form name="order">
<input type="checkbox" name="equipment0"
value="Printer" onClick="setField(this.form)">Printer
<input type="text" name="quantity0" value="1" size=2
onChange="setField(this.form)">
<br>
<input type="checkbox" name="equipment1"
value="Mouse" onClick="setField(this.form)">Mouse
<input type="text" name="quantity1" value="1" size=2
onChange="setField(this.form)">
<br>
<input type="checkbox" name="equipment2"
value="Keyboard"
onClick="setField(this.form)">Keyboard
<input type="text" name="quantity2" value="1" size=2
onChange="setField(this.form)">
<br>
<textarea onChange="setField(this.form)" name=order
value="?" rows=5></textarea>
<br>
</form>
```

When the box is checked, the quantity appears in the text area along with the item name, as long as the quantity of the item is greater than 0.

Question 95: CF Query to JS Array Forms Problem

I'm loading up a JS Array with a Cold Fusion query and that works fine. However, when I try to get the resulting JavaScript array into a form for output it doesn't work.

Here's a URL where you can see what happens: http://www.cfug-vancouver.com/testarray.cfm

Here's the code:

```
<code>
<html>
<head>
  <title>Untitled</title>
</head>
  <CFQUERY name="getnames" datasource="cfug1">
  SELECT id, number, rannumber, visits, password,
firstname, lastname, city,
provstate, country, email, organization,
clientaddress, clientbrowser, url,
listserv
  FROM Members
  Order by Lastname
</CFQUERY>
<body>
<br>
<H1>Test area</H1>
<HR>
<cfoutput>
     <script language="JavaScript">

               //store array for addresses
               var rec_count =
#getnames.recordCount#;
               var id = new Array(rec_count);
               var number = new Array(rec_count);
               var rannumber = new
Array(rec_count);
               var visits = new Array(rec_count);
               var password = new Array(rec_count);
               var firstname = new
Array(rec_count);
               var lastname = new Array(rec_count);
               var city = new Array(rec_count);
               var provstate = new
Array(rec_count);
               var country = new Array(rec_count);
               var email = new Array(rec_count);
               var organization = new
Array(rec_count);
               var clientaddress = new
Array(rec_count);
               var clientbrowser = new
Array(rec_count);
               var url = new Array(rec_count);
               var listserv = new Array(rec_count);
               <cfset count = 0>
               <cfloop query="getnames">
                    number[#count#]= "#number#";
                    rannumber[#count#]=
```

127

```
"#rannumber#";
                              firstname[#count#]=
"#firstname#";
                              lastname[#count#]=
"#lastname#";
                              city[#count#]= "#city#";
                              provstate[#count#]=
"#provstate#";
                              country[#count#]=
"#country#";
                              email[#count#]= "#email#";
                              organization[#count#]=
"#organization#";
                              url[#count#]= "#url#";

                              <cfset count = count +1>
                    </cfloop>
</cfoutput>
//Now the function that is caused by an onchange()
from a select box
//JS event:
            function changeAddress(obj){
                              var j =
obj.selectedIndex - 1;
                              with
(document.displaymembers){
                              firstname.value =
firstname[j];
                              lastname.value =
lastname[j];
                              number.value =
number[j];
                              rannumber.value =
rannumber[j];
                              city.value =
city[j];
                              provstate.value =
provstate[j];
                              country.value =
country[j];
                              email.value =
email[j];
                              organization.value =
organization[j];
                              url.value = url[j];
                              }
        }
</script>
```

```
<font face-"arial, helvetica" size="3" color="navy">
  <form name="displaymembers">
    <select name="getnames"
onchange="changeAddress(this)">
                  <option value="">Personal Addresses
                  <cfif getnames.recordCount gt 0>
                      <cfoutput query="getnames">
          <option value="#id#">#lastname#
                              </cfoutput>
                  </cfif>
                  </select>
                  <br>

<input type="text"  name="firstname" value="">
<input type="text"  name="lastname" value="">
</font>
</form>

</font>
</body>
</html>
</code>
```

How can I make the above code work?

A: Just delete:

```
with (document.displaymembers) {
```

and place in all lines something like the following:

```
document.displaymembers.firstname.value = firstname;
(you have name conflict)
```

Question 96: Delete Elements from an Array

I have a simple phone book with a select box that displays the person's first name and last name (there are about 4 entries in this select box), which it picks up from the (phonedb) array. It then displays this information in 2 text boxes called Firstname, and lastname. I have a button called remove and when I click on this, I want it to delete the selected elements from the array.

How do I write my code?

A: This should work on the newer browsers:

```
<script language="javascript">
 var arrItems = new Array("Item 0", "Item 1", "Item
2", "Item 3", "Item 4")
 document.write("Before removal of Item 2: " +
arrItems + "<br>")

//-----------------This removes stuff
 var arrDummy = arrItems.splice(2,1); /splice(start
at index,number of items) place removed stuff in
arrDummy
//----------------

 document.write("After removal of Item 2: " +
arrItems + "<BR>")
</script>
```

Question 97: Duplicate Browser "Stop" Button with JavaScript

I need to stop loading the rest of the current page when users click on a particular image on the page. Is there a way to duplicate the browser's "Stop" button with JavaScript?

A: This can be done in JavaScript but it has to be done in different ways to accomodate Netscape vs. IE. In Netscape, you simply use the command *window.stop()*. IE might return an error from this command. At the very least, it will not work. With IE, you have to use the command *document.execCommand('Stop')* instead. You'll probably have to build in a browser check to make it work for everyone.

Question 98: Get an Undefined out of the Array

I am using the following code to cycle through the objects in an array I have established:

```
function listGlosNames(obj) {
 var names = "";
 for(var i in obj) names += "<a href='test.htm?key="
+ i + "'>" + i + "</a><br>";
 document.write(names);
}
```

When I call the function from the code, it writes all of the objects but then includes an undefined at the bottom of the list. In a further test, I added an alert to the end of the function after document.write(names). The alert pops up after the last object is written, but before the undefined. Once you click on Ok, the undefined is written to the page. How do I get around this?

A: The following will let you know whether a particular i is undefined:

```
if(typeof(i)!="undefined")
```

Question 99: Imagemap Form Won't Submit

I can't get an imagemap form to submit when the user clicks on a hotspot. It will work in IE 5.5 using DblClick, but in all other cases it doesn't execute. No errors, just nothing happens. The test page is at http://www.mltn.org/search/counties/map_search_test.html

The code in question is:

```
onClick="window.document.mapsearch.submit();"
```

What is causing this problem?

A: Watch what happens if you change it to look like this:

```
<MAP NAME="searchablemap">
    <AREA COORDS="1,0,48,25" ALT="Falmouth"
SHAPE="rect"
        HREF="javascript:getsearchresults();"
        onMouseover="document.forms.mapsearch.lookfor
.value = 'Falmouth';
        return false;"
        >

    <AREA COORDS="2,26,48,50" ALT="Rockland"
SHAPE="rect"
        HREF="javascript:getsearchresults();"
        onMouseover="document.forms.mapsearch.lookfor
.value = 'Rockland';
        return false;"
        >

</MAP>
```

Just put your onclick behavior in the href, and get rid of the onclick. This will work in IE 5.5, NS 6, 4.7 and 3.

Question 100: Command Prompt

```
<script language="javascript">
<!--
var name=window.prompt("plz give me your
name","Fred");
window.confirm("Is " + name + " correct?");
//-->
</script>
```

I want a certain line of code to run when the user clicks ok in the command prompt box, but if he clicks cancel, then a different line of code will be run. How can I write the code so that when the user enters his name, the command box comes up?

A: Try the following:

```
c = window.confirm("Is " + name + " correct?");

if (c)
{
    alert("i'm glad that is correct");
}
else
{
    prompt("Well, what is it then?", "");
}
```

Question 101: Page Refresh With Frames

I am having a problem with this JSP page. I have created a dynamic chat button that when clicked produces a pop-up window that accesses a JSP file from my server and creates a login page on the users window in the pop-up window.

I have also incorporated a script that replaces the original window with a similar page with a tracking script in it when the button is clicked and displays the pop-up window. I have incorporated the script into a JSP file on my server.

When you click the button and the pop-up window displays, the browser replaces the page but it does so in the top frame of the original page instead of the whole page being replaced.

Here is the part of the JSP file that displays my script.

```
// Define the JavaScript code that displays the live
button
StringBuffer liveHelpJS = new StringBuffer();
liveHelpJS.append ( "document.write('<a href=\"#\"
onClick=\"MM_openBrWindow(\\'http://loginpage.jsp?poo
lname=";+poolName+"\\' " );

liveHelpJS.append (
",\\'livedemo\\',\\'resizable=yes,width=400,height=40
0\\')\">" );

liveHelpJS.append ( "<img src=\"image.gif\"
onClick=\"location.replace(\\'http://www.MyURL.com\\'
)\" border=\"0\">" );

liveHelpJS.append ( "</a>');\n" );
</code>
```

I am assuming that the location.replace is replacing the image in the frame instead of the whole page because it is connected to the image. How can I get around this?

A: Use parent.location.replace().

Question 102: JavaScript and ASP with Frames

There is an ASP document with 2 frames (fr1 and fr2).

fr1 --> It has a big form in which there is a select box giving member names from a MS Access DataBase. I have kept the value attribute as the ID of members

DataBase-->the fields are ID, Name, Address.

fr2-->it is a plain document with nothing on it.

I want the Address of the selected name on fr2 when the user selects a name in the fr1 select box. The fr1 should not get REFRESHED at any cost as the user can continue filling the rest of the long form and will get the address of member on fr2 after sometime with the help of JavaScript.

How can I achieve this?

A: onChange of the selectbox, reload frame2 with a querystring of some sort:

```
onChange='parent.frames[1].location="findaddress.asp?
name=" + this.value'
```

In findaddress.asp, have a client-side script to tell the user the address.

Question 103: Change URL Icon

How can I set the icon to appear in the Address field?

A: This only works on IE5+.

First, you have to create a 16x16 pixel ico file. Get an icon editor to do this as I think ico is a special file type that requires special headers. It may just be a bmp though so you can use MS Paint. There are also shareware editors you can download.

You can make a default icon for your whole site by naming it favicon.ico and putting it in your root web directory. Or you can make a per-page icon by using a link tag:

```
<HEAD>
  <LINK REL="SHORTCUT ICON"
HREF="http://domain.com/icon.ico">
  <TITLE>My Title</TITLE>
</HEAD>
```

Your visitors must add your site to their Favorites before they will see the icon appear in the address bar or the favorites menu.

Question 104: Size Images for Different Resolutions

I have images (jpeg) of a certain size that I do not want to roll off the screen. Is there a way to determine the resolution size that someone uses on his or her computer or do I have to create my images to a standard small size?

A: You can dynamically alter the size of your images using CSS:

```
myimageid.style.height=somevalue :IE (not sure about
NS)
```

You can get the screen height/width:

```
screen.height/screen.width          :IE
screen.availHeight/screen.availWidth :NS
```

but the best way to do it is just make your images small enough or send them to a different (less fancy) page with a notification about their resolution.

Question 105: Access Properties of a Cell Table

How can I access the properties of a cell table, e.g., clicking a button such that the cell color changes?

A: In IE:

```
<td id="unf"></td>

<button
onclick="unf.style.backgroundColor='#336699'"></butto
n>
```

Question 106: Select Options in Dropdown Menu

I am testing a form with the following:

```
<form method="POST" name="form" action="--WEBBOT-
SELF--">
  <p><select size="4" name="list" class="daf">
    <option selected value="sfsdf">sfsdf</option>
    <option value="s">asdfasdf</option>
    <option value="asdfsadf ">asdfsadf</option>
    <option value="sadfasdf">sadfasdf</option>
    <option
value="asdfsadfsadf">asdfsadfsadf</option>
    <option
value="asdfsadfasdf">asdfsadfasdf</option>
    <option value="ssadfsadf ">ssadfsadf </option>
  </select></p>
  <p><input type="button" onclick="highlight();"
value="Button" name="B1"></p>
</form>
```

How do I make all of the options in the box highlighted when the button is clicked?

A: Do two things to make it work:

1. Set the select box to "multiple":

```
<select size="4" name="list" class="daf" multiple>
```

2. Paste the following script into your source:

```
<script language="Javascript">
    function highlight() {

    for(j=0; j < document.form.list.length; j++) {
        document.form.list[j].selected=true;
        }
    }
</script>
```

Question 107: Form Won't Submit

I want to be able to submit a form when a user clicks on a link and not via a submit button. The link code is shown here:

```
<a href="#" onClick="setParams('dev')">Houses</a>
```

The setParams function has the following line of code at the end to perform the submit where the form name is ztsuppform.

```
document.ztsuppform.submit();
```

However, this does not submit the form. How do I solve this problem?

A: The following code wil work:

```
<a href="javascript:setParams('dev')">Houses</a>
```

Question 108: Pass Variables from One Frame

Let's say I have two frames with my script in the one on the "left", and if I put the field on the "left", and update it on the "right", its value always comes up null. If i put it on the "right", the update works, but the first time it dies as an undefined object. Is there a way to trap undefined objects or a better way to pass variables?

A: You can access a variable in another frame like so:

```
parent.framename.thing_you_want
```

or

```
parent.frames[frameindex].thing_you_want
```

or

```
parent.frames["framename"].thing_you_want
```

Question 109: Check All Checkbox Controls in a Page

I have an unknown number of checkbox controls, and I have a button control. All I need is to check all the checkbox controls when I click the button control.

How do I do this?

A: You want to loop through them all and set their checked attribute to true. To do this, you would need to number them, and access through document.formName[] array.

You could also make them into radio buttons, and access them through their own array if you wish.

Or you could go through the entire form, asking each element what its type is, and if it returns checkbox, set the value for checked.

```
for(var j =
0;j<document.formName.elements.length;j++){

    if(document.formName.elements[j].type ==
'checkbox'){
        document.formName.elements[j].checked=true;

}
```

Question 110: Scrolling Text

How do I make scrolling text in the status bar?

A: This is what you want:

```
<script language="JavaScript">
<!--
function scrollit_r21(seed)
{
var msg=" Just replace this message with what you
want to say....You can add as much as you want but
try to keep it short so your visitors do not get
bored and impatient like you are now";
var out = " ";
var c = 1;
if (seed > 100) {
seed--;
var cmd="scrollit_r21(" + seed + ") ";
timerTwo=window.setTimeout(cmd, 100) ;
}
else if (seed <= 100 && seed > 0)
{
for (c=0 ; c < seed ; c++)
{
out+=" ";
}
out+=msg;
seed--;
var cmd="scrollit_r21(" + seed + ") ";
window.status=out;
timerTwo=window.setTimeout(cmd, 100) ;
}
else if (seed <= 0)
{
if (-seed < msg.length)
{
out+=msg.substring(-seed,msg.length) ;
seed--;
var cmd="scrollit_r21(" + seed + ")";
window.status=out;
timerTwo=window.setTimeout(cmd, 100) ;
}
else {
window.status=" ";
timerTwo=window.setTimeout("scrollit_r21(100)",75);
```

```
}
}
}
-->
</SCRIPT>

<body onLoad="timerONE=window.setTimeout
('scrollit_r21(100) ' ,500) ;">
</body>
```

Question 111: Capture Value of Variable

```
<%
  gotUID = Session("UID")
%>

<body bgcolor="#FFFFFF">
<center>
<h1>Documentation - B/L</h1>
</center>

<input type="text" name="gotUID"
value="&&#91;gotUID] ">
```

Note the lines:

```
gotUID = Session("UID")
<input type="text" name="gotUID"
value="&&#91;gotUID] ">
```

What do I need to take the value that is returned by the first line and insert it into the second line?

A: This should work:

```
<%
  gotUID = Session("UID")
%>

<body bgcolor="#FFFFFF">
<center>
<h1>Documentation - B/L</h1>
```

```
</center>

<input type="text" name="gotUID" value="<%=gotUID%>">
```

Question 112: Return to Form After "OK" on Alert Box

I have a form where I want users to check a box to confirm that they understand the terms of the upload area. If they fail to check the box, they will be alerted upon clicking the upload button.

```
function validate(form) {
 if (document.UploadForm.controlled.checked)
{
     return true;
}
 else{
     (alert("You must check the box to continue"));
   return false;
 }
 }
```

The alert box comes up correctly. However, if you click okay on the alert box, the upload continues. I want the user to be returned to the form to check the box. How do I correct this problem?

A: In your form, use:

```
<form onsubmit="return validate()">
```

Question 113: Auto Focus Text Box

On my form, I have myphone number field broken into 3 text boxes.

1 - area code = txtArea
2 - first 3 digits = txtPhone1
3 - last 4 digits = txtPhone2

After the user fills the area code field, which has a length equal to 3, I want to automatically set the focus to the next text box.

```
<input type="text" name="txtArea"
onkeypress="if(this.length
==3){document.frmName.txtPhone1.focus()}">
```

What is wrong with my code?

A: Use the following:

```
onkeypress="if(this.value.length ==
3){document.frmName.txtPhone1.focus()}"
```

Question 114: Arrays

```
birthdayarray = new Array(12);
    birthdayarray[0] = "January";
    birthdayarray[1] = "January";
    birthdayarray[2] = "February";
    birthdayarray[3] = "March";
    birthdayarray[4] = "April";
    birthdayarray[5] = "May";
    birthdayarray[6] = "June";
    birthdayarray[7] = "July";
    birthdayarray[8] = "August";
    birthdayarray[9] = "September";
    birthdayarray[10] = "October";
    birthdayarray[11] = "November";
    birthdayarray[12] = "December";

var searchstring = prompt("What number of month were
you born in?","");

for (m=0; m<birthdayarray.length; m++){
    alert(m);
    if (birthdayarray[m].search(searchstring) != -1){
    alert("You were born in "+birthdayarray[m]+",
which is month "+m+" out of 12.")
    }
}
```

What is this code doing from the "for" statement down? Also, how would I rewrite it so that after the users enter their number, the alert box comes up and tells them what month it corresponds to, without having to count to 12?

A: Your code gets the entered text at the prompt and then goes through the array of birthdays.

At every iteration, the array entry is comparing itself to the searchstring. If this does not match then -1 is returned. So if the string in the array[m] entry is the same as the one given as 'searchstring', the alert message is given. The search is just a pattern-matching device.

If you want the alert box to come up, simply get rid of the first *alert(m).*

Question 115: Conversion From String to int

How do I convert string to int in JavaScript?

A: There are three that I am familiar with, assuming x is a string:

```
x=window.parseInt(x)
```

||

```
x=new Number(x)
```

||

```
x=x/1
```

Question 116: Form Validation Based on "True" Field

I am creating a form that will validate "true" fields based on an initial checkbox that was checked at the beginning. If the checkbox is unchecked, the validation does not occur.

I have created the code that can verify "true" values in each of the form elements that I am going to use. I have created a separate code that loops to check if a certain checkbox was checked. Both work fine when I test them independently.

However, when I put the "checkform" function into the "pick" function, I get errors which state that the objects in my "checkform" sub-functions are "null or not an object."

Here is the script:

```
<HTML>
<HEAD>
<TITLE>test</TITLE>
```

```
<SCRIPT language = "JavaScript">
function pick(frm)
{
if(frm.rad[0].checked == true)
{
alert("Checkbox " + 1 + " is checked.\n");return
checkform(this.form)
}

}

function validString(str)
{
if (str.length != 0)
return true
else
return false
}

function getSelectvalue(list)
{
var listval = list.options[list.selectedIndex].value
return listval
}

function countchecks(form)
{
var numboxes = 4
var count = 0

for (i = 0; i < numboxes; i++) {
var newbox = eval("form.box" + i)
if (newbox.checked)
count++
}
return count
}

function ischecked(paytype)
{
for (i = 0; i < paytype.length; i++)
{
if (paytype.checked)
return true
}
return false
}

function checkform(form)
{
```

149

```
if(validString(form.fullname.value) == false)
{
alert("Please provide us with your full name")
form.fullname.focus()
return false
}


fee = getSelectvalue(form.memberlist)
if (fee == 0) {
alert("Please choose a membership category")
form.memberlist.focus()
return false
}


var numcks = countchecks(form)

if (numcks < 1) {
alert("Please choose a box")
return false
}

if (!ischecked(form.payment))
{
alert("Please choose a payment method")
return false
}
{
alert("Data is valid!")

}


}
</SCRIPT>
</HEAD>
<BODY>
<DIV CLASS="top">
<p> </p>
</DIV>
<P> Fill out the form below</P>
<FORM>
<TABLE width="400">
<TR>
<TD>Would you like to join?
<p> Yes:
<INPUT TYPE="checkbox" NAME="rad">
<INPUT TYPE="hidden" NAME="rad">
</p>
</TD>
</TR>
```

```
<TR>
<TD class="rght"><I>*Full Name</I></TD>
<TD class="lft">
<INPUT type="text" name="fullname" size="30" >
</TD>
</TR>
<TR>
<TD>select</TD>
<TD>*
<SELECT name = "memberlist">
<OPTION value = 0> Select a membership category
<OPTION value = 100> Family - $100
<OPTION value = 75> Individual - $75
<OPTION value = 50> Senior - $50
<OPTION value = 30> Youth - $30
</SELECT>
</TD>
</TR>
</TABLE>
<BR>
<TABLE WIDTH=600>
<TR>
<TD COLSPAN=2>
<B>Check all that apply.</B> </TD>
</TR>
<TR>
<TD>
<INPUT type= checkbox name = "box0">
check one<BR>
<INPUT type= checkbox name = "box1">
check two<BR>
<INPUT type= checkbox name = "box2">
check three<BR>
<INPUT type= checkbox name = "box3">
check four<BR>
</TD>
<TD BGCOLOR="silver"> <B>*Choose your method of
payment.</B> <BR>
<INPUT type= radio name = "payment">
Credit card<BR>
<INPUT type= radio name = "payment" >
Bill me<BR>
</TD>
</TR>
</TABLE>
<BR>
<!--Submit button-->
<INPUT type = "button" value = "Submit Form" onClick
= "return pick(this.form)">
<!--Reset button-->
```

```
<INPUT type = "reset" value = "Reset Form">

</FORM>

</BODY>
</HTML>
```

How do I correct the errors?

A: If this section in your code is the initial checker for validation, when the checkbox is checked, the code is supposed to continue. If not, validation should stop.

```
function pick(frm){
    if(frm.rad[0].checked == true){

        alert("Checkbox " + 1 + " is
checked.\n");return checkform(this.form)
    }
  }
```

You are using *this* in "*return checkform(this.form)* improperly. The "this" keyword has no relevance there. It does not refer to the checkbox, so try using:

```
return checkform(frm);
```

"this" refers to the current object, so we use it only inside the tags which define objects, or in the constructors for 'new' ones, it enables us to indicate internal methods or data members.

Question 117: Code Won't Work in Netscape

I have the following script on a Photo Gallery Page:

```
<SCRIPT LANGUAGE="JavaScript">
   function popupPage(pic, w, h)
   {
   var windowprops = "location=no, scrollbars=no,
menubars=no, toolbars=no, resizable=no" + ",left=300,
top=90" + ", width=" + w + ", height=" +
h;
   popup = window.open(pic,"MenuPopup",windowprops);
   }
</SCRIPT>
```

Then I use the following in the body:

```
<A
onClick="popupPage('images/stage.jpg','320','250')"><
IMG BORDER="0" SRC="images/tnstage.jpg" width="75"
height="56"></a>
```

This works in IE, but does not work in Netscape. How do I make it work in both?

A: You have to fix your code a little:

1. Remove all whitespaces in this string:

```
var windowprops =
"location=no,scrollbars=no,menubars=no,toolbars=no,re
sizable=no" + ",left=300, top=90" + ",width=" + w +
",height=" + h;
```

2. Add HREF attribute to <A>:

```
<A href="#"
onClick="popupPage('images/stage.jpg','320','250')"><
IMG BORDER="1" SRC="" width="75" height="56"></a>
```

It works in IE, Opera, NN4.x, and N6.

Question 118: Determine if a User Leaves My Domain

How can I determine if a user leaves mydomain?

A: The following works only in I E 5+, but it only works if the user clicks on a link in your page to leave your site.

```
<html>
<head>
    <title>Untitled</title>
    <script>
    function init()
    {
        var s = document.getElementsByTagName("A");
        for(var i = 0; i < s.length; i++)
        {
            s[i].attachEvent("onclick",
function(){if(this.hostname !=
document.location.hostname){var c = confirm('Are you
sure you want to leave my site?');if(!c){return
false;}}});
        }
    }
</script>
</head>

<body onload="init()">
<a href="http://www.aavex.com/">sdfsdfs</a>
<a href="http://www.aavex.com/">sdfsdfs</a>
<a href="http://www.aavex.com/">sdfsdfs</a>
<a href="http://www.aavex.com/">sdfsdfs</a>
<a href="http://www.aavex.com/">sdfsdfs</a>
<a href="http://www.aavex.com/">sdfsdfs</a>
</body>
</html>
```

With a little bit of tweaking, it might work in Mozilla/NS6 as well.

Question 119: Post Current Browser URL to A Form

I have a simple survey html form that exists on multiple pages throughout a site. I am trying to use JavaScript to assign the value of the current URL (as it exists in the browser's address window—not from the html code of the page) to a hidden variable so it can be passed to the form processing cgi and recorded in a logfile.

How do I write the code?

A: Use this:

```
document.formname.hiddenelement.value =
window.location
```

Question 120: Cancel a mouseClick

I have a submit button:

```
<input type="submit" name="sub1" onclick="checkIt()">
```

How do I cancel the mouse click inside the function checkIt() in case some condition is true (e.g., some data is missing)?

A: Put checkIt in the onsubmit of the form instead:

```
<form name="benluc" action="benluc.asp"
onsumbit="return checkIt()">
```

then just have checkIt return false at any point that is bad.

Index

www.ingramcontent.com/pod-product-compliance
Lightning Source LLC
LaVergne TN
LVHW042335060326
832902LV00006B/194